*To Janet Carter
My High School Friend!
Thank You So Much
Mitch McC 2013*

Radio Daze

1970 - 1976

By Mitch McCracken

Cover design by: Sarah Hascher

Published by Cracker Box Publishing
Copyright December 2011 Mitch McCracken, All rights reserved.
No part of this book may be reproduced, stored or
transmitted by any means without the
written permission of the author.

To my children Justin and Randee;
To Ronnie, Terri and Marsha for their camaraderie and understanding
To Dale and Donna Franklin for their emotional and financial support
To Veronica Marshall, Rickey and Dinah Townsend, Marty Gaines,
Margie Strain, Melissa Brandon-Smith, Andy Tanas, Jon Scott,
Rich and Marsha Boren, Leesa Lewis and Gary Guthrie
for their encouragement as I wrote this book

Table of Contents

Preface	09
Chapter 1: Tears of a Clown	11
Chapter 2: Shelter From the Storm	35
Chapter 3: You've Got a Friend	51
Chapter 4: Teacher	57
Chapter 5: The End of Innocence	67
Chapter 6: Tell Her About It	87
Chapter 7: The Last. DJ	97
Chapter 8: Welcome to My Nightmare	113
Chapter 9: Alone	131
Chapter 10: Against All Odds	139
Chapter 11: Going Down	157
Chapter 12: The City of New Orleans	171
Chapter 13: The Pretender	183
Chapter 14: Free Bird	193
Chapter 15: All The Young Girls Love Alice	203
Chapter: 16: Memphis in the Meantime	217

Radio Daze

Preface

Take a behind the scenes look at what radio was really like in the seventies through the eyes of a Memphis DJ. Read firsthand accounts of some of the seventies biggest stars, including a rather interesting 1974 interview with Jim Morrison, just three years after his death.

This book is about my experiences in radio but I also look back at my childhood giving you an idea of what life was like growing up in a tough Memphis neighborhood called Frayser. My mother's abuse is one of the challenges I faced growing up. In school I became the class clown, always laughing and having fun.

I also write about the many influential people I met along the way; teachers, girlfriends, Program Directors, radio station owners, record company executives, etc. One of the most difficult things about writing this book was telling the story of how a girlfriend was raped by a serial rapist. You will read about what happened to her and how she dealt with it. How it not only affected her life, but mine as well.

I have been a DJ for most of my adult life. In fact, I played classic rock before it was classic. At the time, it was just rock.

I also go into detail about how my magazine, Radio Magazine, was embezzled by Stax Records and Union Planters Bank. I ended up being wrongfully arrested for check fraud. I helped the Attorney General, Hugh Stanton, in his investigation into the bank and one of its officials.

Radio Daze takes a lighthearted look at some serious issues, but mostly the good times. It also gives you a inside look at what it was like to be a disc jockey in the seventies. Radio was fun then, much different from the radio of today.

My life has been one adventure after another. Through the years there have been many people who have inspired and encouraged me. Sit back, get comfortable and let me tell you about some of them.

I hope you enjoy reading Radio Daze as much I did living it...

Chapter one:
Tears of a Clown

I have been a happy person all my life. Sometimes I wonder why. My childhood was pretty miserable, but I never let on. In fact I was the class clown in high school. I guess I still am. I just have no class. I discovered that I had a gift for making people laugh and I enjoyed the hell out of that.

I decided in the ninth grade that I wanted to be a disc jockey and that I did. I loved going to work every day. The life of a DJ is never boring. It was like getting paid for having fun.

I must admit though, it hasn't always been easy being happy, especially when I was growing up. It takes focus, drive and the ability to tune some things out completely.

The first woman I ever loved mistreated me for years. She intentionally hurt me and seemed to enjoy it. I forgave her for all the heartache she brought into my life and continued to love her regardless of how she treated me. I know it sounds crazy until I tell you that she was my mother. She is the most mean spirited person I have ever known.

There's a line in the movie, *The Mirror Crack'd* that reminds me so much of my mother. Elizabeth Taylor plays an actress and at one point she looks at her rival played by Kim Novak and in a very sweet, soft voice says "There are just two things I don't like about you" then her face intensifies as she snarls "Your face." That's my mother, to people who don't really know her it appears as if butter wouldn't melt in her mouth, but at home the demons come out. Mother makes Joan Crawford in "Mommy Dearest" look like June Cleaver.

My home life as a child was full of hate, anger and tension. I saw how when my Uncle Gerald and Aunt Faye were around, the tension between my parents seemed to dissipate. Uncle Gerald could make you laugh at the drop of a hat and on occasion, his pants. They had two sons, Jerry and Kenny and we saw them almost every weekend. Our families even went on vacations together. It was hard for Mother to be mean when she was laughing her butt off. So when I was at school, I became the class clown. My uncle had shown me that humor was the best way to ease tension. I had no control of my life at home, so as soon as I stepped out of the house it was "show time." At school, I took complete control. I made everybody laugh. There were no rules or limitations.

I have two sisters and a brother who shared in my life of misery at the hands of a self-centered, self-serving, and unlikable bitch of a mother. I know, it sounds harsh but you'll see. My brother was my best friend and co-defendant in most cases. My sisters? Well, they were just girls and at the time the enemy for the most part. Ronnie was fifteen months older than me. My sister Terri was sixteen months younger and Marsha was three years behind her.

Chapter 1: Tears of a Clown

Terri was a pretty blonde and as close to being a perfect child as you could get. She always tried to do what was expected of her. She was the people pleaser, or at least the parent pleaser. That was her way of flying under Mother's radar.

While Ronnie, Terri and I favor Dad's side of the family, Marsha looked like a little Marie, the spitting image of my mother. Long brown hair, a cute little round face with deep dimples, I hate to admit my little sister was cute, but she was just a little doll. Marsha pretty much got whatever she wanted, especially from Dad. She did it so effortlessly too. All she had to do was give him a sad puppy look and if that didn't make him crumble like a house of cards, crying would always do the trick. The girls pretty much stayed out of harm's way.

Gene and Marie McCracken

The kids all got along for the most part. It was my parents that were always fighting. They argued often and loudly. I remember my mother's nightly critiques of my dad, his job, his life, his family and his manhood. She did it so loudly that the neighbors were also enlightened to Dad's short comings.

My parents looked like Yogi and Boo Boo. My dad was six foot three and my mother barely five feet tall. As you might imagine she had auburn red hair (dyed) and was quite attractive until you got to know her.

Every night I would shut our bedroom door. Ronnie and I shared one bedroom and the girls another. We turned the fan on high to drown out her constant bitching.

The fan was loud and when that cool air hit me it was like "Calgon take me away." It was like she wasn't even there. I could ease into a deep sleep. As a child I was a very deep sleeper because I wasn't just sleeping, I was hiding.

My dad's biggest mistake was that he really loved my mother and she knew it. She pushed his buttons like a kid on an elevator. Of her four children, three don't speak to her. The other is just too kind hearted to cut her off. None of her brothers or sisters speak to her, nor did my grandmother who recently passed away at nearly a hundred. I'm not sure how old exactly because we were never allowed to have a relationship with her. It seems Grandma didn't get along very well with Mother.

Living like that didn't do a lot for our self-esteem or confidence so Ronnie and I couldn't care less about our grades. We had no self-esteem and therefore no shame. We knew nothing we did would ever please her. If we did, she would just raise the bar. That bothered Ronnie a

Chapter 1: Tears of a Clown

lot more than it did me. I gave up trying at an early age. When guys at school tried to provoke me into a fight by calling me a son of a bitch, I just thought they knew her. When I said "Oh you've met her" everyone would laugh and the tension was gone. Thanks Uncle Gerald.

Terri was the one who made good grades. Mother threw that up to Ronnie and me every chance she got. We each handled the way we grew up very differently. We were disrespected so much by Mother that Ronnie wouldn't take it from anybody else. He got into a lot of fights and stayed mad all the time. While I just tried to make light of it, I ignored all the negativity and grabbed what enjoyment I could out of life. At home there wasn't much to hold onto.

If one of us got into trouble, we both did. It was never Ronnie or Mitch; it was always "the boys." If one of us did something, it was assumed the other was also involved. I think we bonded a lot more because of that. More than if we had a happy childhood, he was the rebel and I was the comedian. I think I enjoyed my humor more than anyone else. It wasn't jokes as much as observations. I have always had the ability to amuse myself, and I do it often and usually at my own expense.

Mother told us on a daily basis we were lazy and stupid. I believed that. Kids believe what their parents tell them. If anybody else says it, it's just their opinion. But if your parent says it, it's a fact. So I saw myself as lazy, stupid and worthless for years.

It was like I was two different people. At home she controlled my every move. She would have controlled my thoughts too if she could. While at home I may have been viewed as worthless, but at school I was the guy who saw the world through rose colored glasses, who enjoyed life to the fullest and encouraged those around me to do the same.

I have a lot of love in my heart and I give it openly and willingly, maybe too willingly. I think it's because I wasn't shown very much love growing up. So I have an unquenchable thirst to give and receive as much love and happiness as possible. I have always worn my heart on my sleeve and just didn't have the good sense to roll my sleeves up. I have been told many times that I'm in denial about the effects of my mom's abuse on me. That's not true.

It would have been very easy for me to be negative and bitter because of the way I was treated at home, but I refused to do that. She was trying to break me, to make me the pitiful sad person she wanted me to be. I fought her attempts to transform me at every turn.

My mother's abuse started early in my life. One night I had a cough when I was five or six and I couldn't go to sleep. Mother yelled from her bedroom to "stop faking that cough and go to sleep." She never considered for even a second that I may really have a cold, or heaven forbid the flu. I tried to suppress the cough as best I could. But I couldn't stop as hard as I tried. The next time

Chapter 1: Tears of a Clown

I coughed, I heard her go into the bathroom and open the medicine cabinet. The cough syrup she used tasted atrocious. I was sure it was just for punishment and nothing more. I was hoping she didn't bring it with her.

She wore flip flops and you could hear her flopping down the hall. The faster she walked the madder she was. By the way she was walking I could tell she was really pissed. She came into my bedroom with a jar of Vicks Vapor Rub in her hand. I took a big sigh of relief because she didn't bring the God awful cough syrup. However, the relief was short lived. Instead of rubbing it on my chest she dipped her fingers in the jar, got a big chunk of it. She jerked my head back with a fist full of the hair on the back of my head and shoved it in my mouth. She spread it in a circular motion on my checks, tongue and the top of my mouth.

Me at age 6

I looked up at her in disbelief. The look on her face was so intense and filled with hate and anger. Her jaw was clamped shut so tightly you could see her jaw muscles bulging and her nostrils were flaring with each breath. She was almost hyperventilating. How did I make her so mad just by simply coughing? With her fingers still in my mouth tears started to roll down my face as I tried not to gag. That worked about as well as trying not to cough. I thought I was going to heave so I darted to the bathroom. She started laughing at me. I couldn't even drink water for relief, it just beaded up on the inside of my mouth. I came back to bed still gagging. She left the room as fast as she came in. Over her shoulder and the noise of her flip flops popping she asked "Is that the kind of attention you wanted? NOW, stop coughing and go to sleep." To this day, the smell of anything menthol makes me gag.

About the same age I developed a bad habit of leaving the door open when I had to go to the bathroom. The standing up bathroom run, if I had to sit down I would notice it was open and shut it. I was a kid and with my back to the door I just didn't notice it was open. Mother told me if I did it again I would have to go pee off the front porch, and of course it happened again. She didn't say a word. But the next time I had to go, sure enough she made me go outside so everyone could see me relieve myself from the front porch. If I had been older it may have bothered me but kids that age have no modesty. I enjoyed it; it felt good out...literally. There were ants down there in the dirt and my fire hose was wiping them out, sending them down the amber river. I couldn't wait until I had to go again.

She liked to punish us through embarrassment and pain. Whenever Mother thought I was in need of physical punishment, she would make me go out to the Weeping Willow tree, which I called Whipping Willow for years, in the backyard and cut a switch for her to use on me. If Mother sent you to the backyard to pick the

Chapter 1: Tears of a Clown

means of your lashing, God help you if you picked one that was too small for the job.

I held the switch in one hand and chopped it with a steak knife with the other. I accidently cut my finger. I wacked it pretty good and it started to bleed profusely. I finished cutting the switch and ran in the house. When Mother saw me she screamed "Oh my God," grabbed me up and headed for the bathroom. I'm still not sure if she was worried about me or the living room rug.

Finally she realized that she was asking too much from a little boy I thought. You would think cutting my finger was punishment enough for whatever I did to make her mad. She ran cold water over the cut, and then poured peroxide on it before putting on the Band Aid. She had me take my pants off because I got blood on them and she needed to soak them. "Are you ok?" she asked tenderly. "I am now, thanks Mother," I answered. "Good" she yelled as she started switching my bare legs with the bloody switch I just brought her, with all the vigor and precision of Zorro. The mark of Zorro had nothing on the Switch of the Bitch. The whole time she was telling me what an idiot I was to cut my finger.

When she got mad at us, not only would she hit us but she would also go for days without speaking to us. That really bothered me when I was young, but as I got older I realized it was a blessing.

When she "helped" me with my homework she would

hit me upside the head with the board or slap me in the face if I got an answer wrong. The horror of getting it wrong was much stronger than the glory of getting it right. So in school I would always second guess myself. I was afraid I didn't know the correct answer so I would come up with some wise crack so the teacher would ask someone else. Most of the time if I had just gone with what I thought the answer was, I would have been right.

When your Mother doesn't believe in you it's hard to believe in yourself. I fought hard to make sure my friends never saw me as she did. They saw a guy who was always laughing and having a good time, a guy full of confidence that didn't care what anyone thought of him. Truth be told, what people thought was one of the most important things in the world to me. Humor is what gave me their acceptance. I could never let them see the paranoid, defeated and self-conscious kid I really was. I escaped into a world where I could make people laugh, one where I was liked. A world where happiness replaced anger and laughter replaced hate. I was always happy at school no matter what was going on.

The summer was much worse than the school year. Three months at home with Miss Congeniality seemed like a three year jail sentence with Nurse Ratched as the warden. One summer she bought two of those little plastic water fountains that you hook up to the outside water faucet, one for the front yard and one for the back. That was pretty cool I thought. She hooked them up and told us we could go outside and play. See she wasn't all

Chapter 1: Tears of a Clown

bad, right? Wrong. Then she locked the door leaving us out all day long. She brought sandwiches outside and made us eat out there in the Memphis humid heat. The summer days would get up to ninety five degrees and the humidity was about the same. It was torture. But then she could watch Password, the Dating Game and the Newly Wed game in peace.

When I was growing up, my parents were only home together on Sunday so our weekend consisted of Friday, Saturday, Fightday. They got into an argument every Sunday. One Sunday Mother put a cinder block at the end of the driveway. She went in and started a fight with Dad A-gain. As usual he grabbed his bowling bag, threw it into the car and squealed down the driveway. When he hit the cinder block, it took out his oil pan and she just died laughing. I could just hear her screech "I'll get you and your little dog too." I have never understood why she enjoyed being so damn mean.

Once when Ronnie and I were in high school, she caught us with our shirt tails out. It was the sixties. Everybody wore their shirt tails out. She went into our closet, cut the tails off all our shirts and sewed white sheets on the bottom.

The next night was Friday and we were going to a party at the Wallace's house. Jean Wallace was in between Ronnie and me in age. She had twin siblings, Gale and her brother Dale who where a little younger than I was. Dale was a great guy with two beautiful sisters. Jean was a sweet girl who would do anything in the world for you (within reason). Gale was the bad girl in the family; she looked a lot like Jean but wore shorter skirts and loved pushing the envelope, they reminded me of Samantha and Serena on Bewitched. They always had great parties. I think Ronnie and Jean liked each other, you could see it but neither one admitted it to the other.

The party was going strong and everyone started taking their shirt tails out. Peer pressure demanded we do the same. I looked at Ronnie who was off in the corner talking to Jean and he just shook his head no. I took a big breath and gave it a yank anyway. I knew I had better have a good story for how ridiculous I looked wearing a blue and white checkered shirt with a solid white shirt tail. I knew exactly what I was going to say too.

Remember that dream about being naked in public? How people looked at you in that dream? My friends were looking at me just like that. I said "You guys are so un-cool, where have you been? This is the new style, you autograph the bottom." I looked back at Ronnie. He was still shaking his head but now it was in disbelief and he was laughing so hard he could hardly get his shirt tail out. God bless 'em. He was always my best audience. I had a black magic marker just for the occasion and had everyone sign our shirt tails.

I knew on the way home the punishment was going to be severe but I didn't care. If that was the price I had to

Chapter 1: Tears of a Clown

pay, so be it. It was worth it. It was better to take another beating from Mommie Dearest than to have our friends know how controlling she was. I was determined she wasn't going to get the best of us in front of our friends. That was a recurring theme as far as she and I were concerned. She would try and I would stop her at all costs. So we went home with our shirt tails out and over twenty signatures on each one. She was livid. She thought she had put an end to the shirt tail thing in her oh so clever way. But in a battle of wits with me, she was unarmed.

The signatures weren't so much to show her how clever I was but to demonstrate that she couldn't control me. She would do anything to achieve and maintain complete control of me and the whole family. She had a leather strap and "The Enforcer" to help her. The Enforcer was a paddle of sorts. It was a wooden board about a foot long, four inches wide and half an inch thick. It had black electrical tape wrapped around it about every inch or so. That way it would make whelps when you were hit with it. She counted the signatures on the shirt and hit us as hard as she could for each one.

Another time she told Ronnie to load the shotgun. She had done that once before because she wanted to shoot our dog, Brownie. That time Ronnie knew why she wanted it loaded. He didn't put a shell in. So this time he wasn't sure why she wanted it loaded but she wanted to see the shell was in there. Once she saw the shell she told Ronnie to follow her.

She walked out of the house into the carport. Dad was working in the utility room with his back to her. She aimed the .410 shotgun at the back of his head and yelled "Gene," when he turned around and found himself looking down the barrel of the shotgun. She gave him enough time to realize who was going to shoot him. But before he could say a word, she pulled the trigger. It just clicked but didn't fire. Ronnie had put a spent shell in this time. Dad grabbed the gun and ran after her.

She was so short with little legs and his legs were almost as long as she was tall. It was like Danny Devito trying to outrun Brad Garrett. He caught her a few steps into the front yard. He drug her into the house and turned around to tell Ronnie "No one needs to know about this."

Dad said she had just returned from Houston (my uncle Wayne had just died) and she was upset. Uncle Wayne was the closest to her of all her eight siblings. Dad loved her so much. She just tried to blow his head off, and his first thought was to protect her.

Then there was the time I got a three day suspension for skipping school. Now, think about that a minute. You don't go to school, so your punishment is that you don't have to go to school for three whole days. Hello? This is punishment? In what Bizzaro world does that make sense? Anyway, three days later it was off to school with Cruella De Vil.

Chapter 1: Tears of a Clown

We parked the car and walked by the auditorium to the sidewalk, about four and a half feet from the classroom windows. The windows were open and it was thirty yards or so to the front door. As soon as we got in front of the classrooms Mother grabbed my hand and started skipping down the sidewalk as if we were on the Yellow Brick Road. Again she was trying to embarrass me in front of my friends and classmates. She looked at me and said, "If you fight, it will look worse." She was right. So I got into it. Before I knew it I was ahead of her and she was fighting to keep up with me. I broke into song "We're Off to see the Wizard." I could hear laughter from the classrooms. Backfire, I loved it. I was starting to enjoy the combat because I was winning more and more of the competitions.

Leon "Pop" Stevenson, the Principal was a nice but stern man with a full head of solid white hair, clean shaven with thick black eyebrows that made Andy Rooney's look well groomed. He pointed out to Mother that I had over a hundred detentions already for the year. She got a blank look on her face and said "But I only signed three." Pop Stevenson looked at me with those eyebrows raised and asked "Are those the ones I thought you forged?" "Yes Sir," I said proudly. "I told you that you could call and ask her." My two worlds had just collided, I had the carefree attitude that I was known for at school but I knew there was going to be hell to pay. I got the beating of my life when I got home. She made me strip down to my underwear and she beat me with that board. I had bruises from my shoulders to my ankles that lasted for weeks.

A few days later I was playing around with a friend in spelling class. He tried to grab me and all he got was my shirt. He pulled it up and exposed the bruises on my back. Mrs. Reed, the teacher saw them and reported it to the Guidance Counselor who wanted to turn my parents in for child abuse. I begged him not to. I told him he would just make my situation at home even more unbearable. So he didn't. But he should have.

It was about that time America was invaded by the British. The Beatles had just landed on the east coast and Ronnie and I were among the first at Frayser High School to start growing our hair out. My mother decided that it would be a good idea for us to put Dippity-Do in our hair. Remember Dippity-Do? It was a hair gel product for women. When it dried your hair was stiffer than a thirteen year old boy on a nude beach. That way there would be no combing it down later in the day. Mother would smell my hair every morning to make sure I obeyed her directions. Then every morning just before we left for school I would tell her I had to go to the bathroom. I'd go wash it out of my hair and as soon as I left for school I shook it down to let it dry. Bada Bing Bada Boom, I'm Ringo!

She came home early from work one day and caught us with our hair combed down. She was losing control so she decided that as punishment we should get a GI haircut, you know, a buzz. Her thought was "If you look

Chapter 1: Tears of a Clown

like a student, you will act like a student." The next day when I got to school the first guy to see me said "Hey McCracken, who cut off your personality?" That was it. She had succeeded in embarrassing me. The war was on. I did anything but act like a student. I raised hell in and out of school. I wasn't interested in girls then because I felt like such a dork. I had whiskers on my head instead of hair. It was kind of fun though, I had a shive a git attitude.

There was one exception; I went to school with a girl named Chris. She had waist length, beautiful blond hair. She was very petite with the cutest dimples and beautiful blue eyes. Her eyebrows were dark brown and thick, like Brooke Shields when she was a teenager. She was a cheerleader and I, along with every other guy on the planet had a crush on her.

Chris and I became good friends and I finally worked up the courage to ask her out in the cafeteria one day. When I did, she said "Aw Mitch, I can't go out with you, you're like my brother." I guess she saw the disappointment in my face when she said that and added "Well, you wouldn't go out with your sister, would you?" I just looked at her with a slight grin and said, "If she looked like you I would." I got a laugh, but not a date. The problem with me is whatever goes through my head comes out my mouth. By using that little bit of humor I didn't have to deal with the rejection and it also made her more comfortable. She turned me down but I was happy because I did make her laugh. It made it seem as if I was so confident that being turned down didn't affect me at all. Truthfully I just wanted the floor to open up and swallow me.

The following day I was in music class and the teacher, Miss Clark, was bent over the desk next to me going over the music scale or something. Jerry, a friend of mine and one of the school hoods, was trying to squeeze past Miss Clark's butt and my desk. While most kids were growing their hair out and combing it down, Jerry was still lost in the fifties. He combed his hair back into a ducktail. He wore penny loafers with nickels in them and taps on the heels so they made noise when he drug his heels. He was facing Miss Clark as he tried to squeeze by. When they lined up, I pinched his ass. Jerry poked her right in the butt. It was hilarious. She turned around and ka-pow slapped the crap out of him.

I ended up getting a board suspension for that. Mother sat me down and asked "What am I going to have to do to get you to calm down?" "The only thing I really care about is my hair, just leave my hair alone. You do that for me, and I'll do better in school" I said. To my surprise she agreed that she would let me wear my hair however I wanted if it was okay with the school. God got me for that little deal. I'm bald now.

Whenever she made a promise that she decided she didn't want to keep, she would look for loopholes. Like most of her promises she didn't keep the one about my hair. She snuck into my room one night while I was

Chapter 1: Tears of a Clown

sleeping and cut a big gap in the front of my hair. The idea was that I would be so embarrassed I would run to the barber shop and get it cut. When I asked her about what she had done, she said with a smirk "I told you could wear it however you want, you don't have to get it cut unless you just want to." So I didn't, I wasn't about to give her the satisfaction. I wore it like that until it grew out. I had the first punk haircut in Memphis.

After she married my step father Bob, who like my dad was a great guy, she invited me over for dinner. She was telling Bob how we (her four kids) never got away with anything. She was so shrewd she caught us at every turn. She was so much smarter than her stupid, lazy kids. At that point I had to think of which story I wanted to share. She only knew what she caught us doing but there were many things she missed. Kind of like "I taught you everything you know, but I didn't teach you everything I know."

I decided on the Report Card switch. I said "You never found out about me signing the Report Cards." You could see that blank look come over her face again as she demanded "What the hell are you talking about." I explained "Well I always made pretty good grades the first six weeks, so I had no problem with you seeing my report card. You would sign it and I would go to school and tell my homeroom teacher I lost it. She would issue another one that I signed and turned in the next day. You kept signing the lost one that I filled in and I would sign the real one for the rest of the year. You never found out about that did ya?"

As her face turned red and her nostrils began to flair she headed for the refrigerator for more ice. The silence was deafening and the tension was so thick you could cut it with a knife. She didn't like to be embarrassed in front of Bob. She was behind him and I could see him holding back a laugh as he gave me a wink. He was a great guy and like Dad he saw her for who she was but loved her anyway.

On her way back to the table she grabbed the iron skillet that was always on the stove and popped me in the back of the head with it. I wasn't the cowering little dog anymore. I didn't cry out in pain even though it hurt like hell. My only reaction was to stand up, look her in the eye and say "That's the last time you will ever hit me. Do it again and I'll give you a taste of your own medicine." I looked over at Bob and he held his hands up as if to say this is just between you and your mother.

Bob never butted in, never tried to replace my dad but he did offer good advice and suggestions. I loved Bob. I told him once that I wished he was my real father. Knowing how much I love Dad he asked "Boy, why would you say that?" I laughed and said "Because you have a full head of hair." He gave me a playful slap on the back and started laughing too.

Bob was a lot like Dad in many ways, how in the world did she attract such great men? I was eighteen then and I told her if she didn't change her ways she would die a very lonely woman. She didn't and she will.

Chapter 1: Tears of a Clown

Now she lives in middle Tennessee near Shiloh Civil War Park, which is perfect for her since she's still fighting the war.

Just because we grew up and moved out didn't mean the madness stopped. The venom she spewed could reach out and zap you no matter where you were. My sister Terri has one child and her sun rises and sets on Melinda. The second most important day of Terri's life, second only to Melinda's birth, was Melinda's wedding day. Mother didn't RSVP so when Terri called to see if she was coming to the wedding Mother said "I don't know, it depends on what's happening that day." She did show up though in a muumuu without a stitch of makeup on. She was 72. She refused to speak to Terri all day thereby making the day about her and not Melinda's wedding.

Marsha has also felt the pain of a continuing relationship with the antichrist. When Marsha's daughter Christi was giving birth to her son Mother told her she wanted to come to the hospital to see Christi and her first great grandson, Austin. She went on to say that when she was there Austin's father and Grandfather (Christi's Dad) would not be allowed in the room. She said Marsha could tell them whatever she wanted as long as Mother didn't have to see them.

She's unbelievable, always has been but it seems the older she gets the meaner she becomes. When I was working in Las Vegas I told a coworker about my mother and that she was a bitch. She was shocked and appalled and said, "You can't say that about your own mother!" "Have you ever known a bitch," I asked. "Sure I have" she admitted. "Well, she's somebody's mother."

It was amazing how successful I became after I got away from Mother's influence. Then I realized that her opinion was just that, her opinion. That didn't make it a fact. She was wrong about most things.

Eventually I actually became that happy go lucky guy I was in school, my escape became my reality.

I don't speak to her now because she still talks smack about Dad. They have been divorced for forty two years and he has been dead now for twenty four. I told her it's okay to talk bad about her ex, just not to his kids. She didn't listen.

I asked my mother once why she was so mean and she yelled at me "My mother was mean to me" to which I snapped "So was mine." We just stared at each other for a minute and then with a very sincere look on my face I said "I think I understand why you have been mad at the world all these years." "Why, why is that" she snarled. "Because Dorothy's

With my son Justin

Chapter 1: Tears of a Clown

house landed on your sister" I said with a sly grin.

"That's not funny."

"My friends think it is."

"You call me a witch in front of your friends?"

"Well sounds like" I said and we both started laughing. She thought I was kidding.

They say everything happens for a reason. The only good thing about living with Mother was the flying monkeys. I did learn a lot from living with her though. Not from her mind you, but from living with her. I learned to never go to bed angry at your spouse or your children. Hold your tongue until you are no longer angry. Never call anyone you love names. When the punishment is over, let your child know that you are not mad at them and that you love them. Don't just tell them when they do something wrong, praise them for what they do that is right as well.

My little girl Randee

So, if you are one of those women who judge men by how they treat their mother. Take the time first to find out about her. Kids do believe what their parents tell them. Before you speak, remember it takes a thousand atta boys to make up for one stupid. The cycle ends with her. I told my kids as they were growing up I love them and that they are good people, because I do and they are. I forgive my mother for what she has done to me and my family. But by forgiving her, it doesn't mean I want her in my life, it just means I have no hate in my heart for her.

Negativity is a waste of time and energy. In fact, it was Bob who helped me understand her a little better. He asked me once "Mitch, do you know what's wrong with your Mother?" "Numerically or alphabetically" I asked. He laughed and said "No, it's just one thing. She thinks everyone should have her morals and values. If they don't they're wrong." He was right, but there is a lot more to it than that.

I think happiness is a decision we all make for ourselves. You really do have a choice you know. Do you want to worry about things you can't change, or do you want to accept the hand you're dealt and marvel at what life has to offer?

Chapter Two:
Shelter from the Storm

My Dad was an easy man to admire. He was a very strong man. I mean that both physically and emotionally. He was brave, strong willed and had one hell of a temper. He also had a soft and loving side like few men I have ever known. If he was mad, you knew it. He would say what he needed to say and he was done with it. So his anger never lasted very long.

Dad grew up in a time when men were strong and strong meant you didn't show emotion, be it love or sorrow. "I love you" was very hard for him to say, he didn't say it very often. But when I needed to hear it, he made sure I did. I can still feel his hug and it was never a token hug. It was real. It said what many times he couldn't. It made you feel safe and secure. With Dad on your side nothing could harm you. He was what made life bearable. He could always put a smile on my face. My mother made our family dysfunctional, but Dad was our shelter from the storm. When she would try to tear the family apart, he was the glue that held it together. To me he was ten feet tall and bullet proof. But as Superman had his Green Kryptonite, Dad had my mother.

He only had a third grade education because of hard financial times with his family. Dad had seven brothers and sisters and lived on a farm in Water Valley, Mississippi. He dropped out of school to work the farm. So he wasn't an educated man but he was a very smart man. He graduated with honors from the School of Hard Knocks with a major in common sense.

Dad taught me by example that you could be kind, giving and caring and still be a man in every sense of the word. When he was working in the foundry at International Harvester melting the metal to make parts for the cotton pickers; he would come home dirty, sweaty and tired. Mother was a cashier at Fay Builders Supply across town. Dad got home about an hour and a half before she did. By the time she got there he had showered, dinner was on the table and he met her at the door with her favorite drink, bourbon and Wink (The sassy one from Canada Dry) in his hand. Once I heard her tell him that "Real men don't cook." That didn't faze him at all. He just let her insults and criticism go and continued to be just as loving and giving to her as he could be. That really impressed me.

Ronnie (L), some Bozo who lived down the street and me

On their eighteenth wedding anniversary Dad threw her a surprise party and had eighteen long stem red roses delivered at 8PM. Instead of thanking him she just threw the vase on the hardwood floor in the living room breaking it into pieces in front of all their friends. He looked at the flowers lying on the floor and then at Mother and said "You're welcome?" Even as a kid I could see the pain in his eyes when she would do things like

Chapter 2: Shelter from the Storm

that to him. She did it every chance she got.

Dad could make his point in many ways; spanking us, through example and every so often through humor. Like the time they found out that Ronnie and I were smoking. My mother told Dad to take us into the bedroom and deal with us. I thought we were going to get a beating. He followed us into our room and shut the door. Dad never showed emotion. He was a man's man but as he turned around there was a tear running down his cheek. Like Iron Eyes Cody in the litter commercial. He looked at us and said "Boys, don't do to you what I did to me." That was powerful. I quit that day. Ronnie said he was going to taper off. That was over forty years ago. He's down to a pack a day now.

I asked Dad the next day if he wanted to quit. He kind of chuckled and said "All those people talking about how hard it is to quit smoking, they're all full of crap. It's the easiest thing I've ever done in my life. Hell, I've done it thirteen times." I busted out laughing and then he asked, "You understand what I'm telling you Mitch?" "Yes sir I hear you, I've smoked my last one," and I had.

He chose to make his point with humor. I loved it when he did that and he could never do it too much for me. I remember another time he used humor. It was when Ronnie, who would fight anybody, anytime, anywhere got into another one. I never wanted to fight at all. In high school we both weighed about a buck and a quarter, so the odds were always against us.

Ronnie challenged a guy to a fight over a girl. His name was Billy and he outweighed Ronnie by at least thirty five pounds with two percent body fat. He kept knocking Ronnie down and Ronnie kept getting back up. Ronnie was hitting him plenty of times. They just didn't pack the same punch. The fifth time he got up his eyes rolled back in his head and he fell back to the ground. I had to call Dad to come pick us up. The inside of Ronnie's mouth was like mincemeat and blood was running down his chin. Dad and I shoveled him into the backseat and Dad turned him on his side and put a towel under his cheek.

As we pulled into the driveway Ronnie started to come around a little bit and Dad looked over his shoulder into the backseat and asked "What chew fightin' bout boy?" The inside of his mouth was raw but as best he could he said "someabitch called mah girlfriend a name." With a smile Dad said "Huh, I bet he won't do that again." I couldn't believe it that was so funny. Even Ronnie was laughing, until it hurt. As a matter of fact, Ronnie was comfortable with who he was and what he was like. He made no bones about it. Billy had said something about the girl Ronnie was dating in front of some friends. Even though he was much bigger, in Ronnie's eyes, there was no choice. He had to fight him. It turns out that Billy had called Ronnie's girlfriend the school slut. She was.

It wasn't that Ronnie was mean or stupid. I think it was because of the lack of respect that he got from

Chapter 2: Shelter from the Storm

Mother. He was determined that no one else would disrespect him. When Billy said that, it was a matter of pride and honor for Ronnie. You could be twice his size or have him out numbered but if you disrespected him he would be in your face ready to take you on. He had the heart of a lion. You could beat the crap out of him and he would still keep coming at you. Like the Black Knight in 'The Holy Grail', you could cut his arms and legs off and he would still try to bite you.

I have heard people describe a friend by saying "I love him like a brother," they only say that because they are uncomfortable saying they love another guy and want to make it clear they're not gay, (not that there's anything wrong with that). Well, Ronnie was my brother that I loved like my best friend. We were inseparable growing up and always had each other's back. We used to talk about growing up, getting married and either sharing a big house or maybe a duplex. But we knew even then that we were going to be a big part of each other's life forever.

Even though we were fifteen months apart in age, most people thought Ronnie and I were twins. We played on that as much as possible. We would trade classes just to see if anyone would notice. Some of our classmates knew but the teachers never did.

When we were old enough to date we would go out on double dates. At some point we'd go to the bathroom and trade shirts. I loved doing that.

We had an old Rambler Classic that was like a big metal shoebox on wheels. Ronnie used to drive me and my girlfriend Debi everywhere we went. He didn't mind because driving was new to him and he enjoyed it. The fact that he had a crush on Debi was also a plus. He looked forward to my dates as much as I did. Whenever we would drop her off, as soon as the door shut he would say "I love her Mitch." I thought he was kidding at first, but he really did.

The first day I could drive by myself, Mother asked me to go to the store. Debi didn't live too far from the store so I decided to go by and showoff. No one would be the wiser. Or so I thought.

As I turned the corner by her house I saw her standing on the corner with a couple of her friends. I drove on the left side of the street to get her attention. As I turned the corner in front of her house I looked back to make sure she saw me driving. I was young, dumb and full of...myself. As I looked back like an idiot I slammed into a telephone pole. It dented the front of the car, broke the headlight and the linkage to the accelerator. The car was going twenty five miles an hour without touching the gas pedal. I left some of the white paint from the car on the telephone pole and broken glass on the ground in front of it. I was freaking out and had to get the car back home. I walked around the car assessing the damage quite loudly. Debi's Mother opened the window and said "He cusses doesn't he?" NOT a good first impression.

Chapter 2: Shelter from the Storm

On the way home, every time I needed to stop I had to stand on the brake and the car would eventually slow to a stop. I was almost home and as I came up to the last red light at Frayser Blvd and North Watkins, I had it timed about right. Just then some dumbass effin' biatch pulled out in front of me and BAM, I rear ended her. Hmmm, maybe I do cuss too much.

We pulled over into the Pic Pac parking lot. I was only going about five miles an hour when I hit her. I knew it sounded like I was going a lot faster. There was no damage to either car, except her trailer hitch put a little bitty dent in my license plate. Of course when she got out she was holding her neck. She thought I put the dent in my fender when I hit her. When she found out I didn't, her neck started feeling much better. There were witnesses that could hear there was something already wrong with the Rambler, besides the driver I mean.

I called the Police, the insurance company and my parents. I told everyone that when I was in the store a truck had backed into me, all I was doing was trying to get it home. Everybody bought it without a question. Mother and Dad showed up and I told them the same story. While I was talking to Mother, Dad went and looked at the car.

He walked over to us and said, "Mitch, c'mere a minute. I want to talk to you about the car." As impresssive as his humor was, his street smarts were even more so. We walked over to the car and he said, "Let me tell you what happened ok?" "Sure" I said as I swallowed a lump in my throat the size of a softball. I could tell when he was getting mad because one eyebrow would be raised and the other dropped down. "You went to see your girlfriend and hit a telephone pole by her house." I could feel the blood drain from my face as I listened. I was trying not to show how shocked I was that he knew exactly what happened. "Here's how I know that. Look at the front of the car. It's dented from the top of the hood to the bottom of the bumper that means you hit something vertical" he explained. He had me dead to rights. Then he reached over and scratched the brown stain on the hood, "Here, do you smell that? You know what that is?" he asked.

"No sir."

"That's Creosote, the only thing they put it on is telephone poles." Actually they put it on railroad ties too, but that was no time to play point/counter point. "I'm going to let you go home and I'm gonna go over to Debi's house and find the pole you hit."

When he left I ran to a pay phone and called Debi. I told her to go out and pick up the glass in front of the telephone pole. "What about the paint on it?" she asked. I thought for a second and said "Put a Yard Sale sign on it!" Her mom was having a yard sale that weekend, so she got everything handled before he drove by. He wasn't sure where she lived, just the neighborhood. I told him a few months later he was right on the money and

Chapter 2: Shelter from the Storm

how impressed I was with how he figured it out. He was not pleased that I lied to him. It caused a big fight with Mother who had believed me for once (maybe just because he didn't). Every election she would vote for the opposing candidate just to cancel Dad's vote.

I finally told Ronnie he could have Debi because she was becoming a little controlling. Not only did he start dating her, he married her. Debi became Ronnie's first wife. He has been married five times and their names all started with "D"; Debi, Debbie, Danae, Diane and Diane again. Wife number four and five are the same person so either he realized the error of his ways or made the same mistake twice. Diane says it's the former.

When my parents got into fights they would go on for days. One time when they were fighting about God knows what, Dad tore two plates off the wall my mother had hanging in the hallway. They were made of tin, painted black with yellow roses. He bent them in half and threw them on the floor. He would tear things up in the house to keep from hitting her. I would have preferred he didn't do that.

The next day when he came home from work, Mother had bent them back out and hung them back up again. They were badly dented and wrinkled not to mention the paint was chipping off them. They were not nearly as attractive as before, but they were back on the wall and she had made her point.

That was like drawing the line in the sand to Dad. Ronnie and Dad were a lot alike in that sense. If you challenged him, it was a fight to the end. She didn't know when to stop, she never did. She should've considered the fact that he could easily just put her in his pocket. Anyway, he took them off the wall, bent them over twice this time and threw them back on the floor. Then he went into his bedroom and slammed the door. The house shook when he did that, something like a 6.5 on the Richter scale. They were still on the floor when he left for work the next morning.

When we came home from school that afternoon, we went right to our room and pretended to be doing our homework. We heard Dad when he came in. He went right to the hall and turned on the light. He busted out laughing and called us out of our room to see what was so funny. My mother had bent the plates back out, chipping even more paint off the once very decorative plates, but it didn't matter because she had driven ten penny nails into each one. All you could see were the nail heads and just the rims of the plates, but by God, he wasn't going to take them down again. To this day that hall wall looks like it has acne scars. Dad had a good sense of humor and appreciated hers.

One day my parents sat all four of us down on the couch and said we have to tell you something that's going to be hard to hear. It was like Sonny and Cher's song "You Better Sit down Kids" but instead of being devastated over the impending divorce, we all sprung off

Chapter 2: Shelter from the Storm

the couch cheering for joy.

When my parents finally got their divorce Mother wanted all of us to live with her and she usually got what she wanted either through force or guilt.

I thought about what if I was in Dad's place? How could I handle going from a family of six to living alone? I couldn't. Even though he didn't show it, I knew Dad was hurting. So I talked to Ronnie and we refused to leave him all alone, we didn't think it was fair for him to have no one so we stayed with him while both my sisters went to live with the Sea Hag. Ronnie ended up joining the Air Force to get away from the war at home. That left just me and Dad. Growing up he had always been closer to Ronnie, being the first born they had a stronger bond. This would be my time to bond with him.

Right after they separated when we were still living in the house, I was looking through the cabinets in the kitchen. The big thing at the time was electric frying pans and there it was. Mother had taken about half the house with her but left the electric frying pan. While I was standing there looking into the cabinet Dad walked into the kitchen on his way to the refrigerator to find something for dinner. "Hey Dad, look what Mother left us" I said with delight. As he walked by me he looked down to see what I was so thrilled about, never breaking his stride he said "Hell son, she didn't leave it. She forgot it."

With just me and Dad living there, he decided to put the house up for sale and we moved into an apartment across the street from the high school. It also just happened to be right around the corner from the apartments where Mother and my sisters lived.

It was great; it was like we were roommates. We went out to dinner a lot at Moore's Steak House, which wasn't really a restaurant. It was a bar that served a rib eye steak sandwich. Dad started going out with some of the waitresses who were in their mid to late twenties, he was 56. I asked him once if they thought he had money. "Naw son," he said "It's called the McCracken charm. I got it. You got it. Your brother Ronnie, he don't got it." I knew that Dad was just trying to give us something to bond over, he never talked bad about Ronnie because they were so much alike, Ronnie was "Little Gene." He was right though, Ronnie wasn't charming. He didn't try to be. I was Paul McCartney the happy, witty Beatle. Ronnie was John Lennon the deep, brooding Beatle.

I started to get to know some of the residents at the apartment complex out at the pool. Some of them were older and one of them offered me a drink. At first I refused but eventually I gave in and started to drink, mainly bourbon and coke.

Somehow Dad found out about it, but to my surprise he wasn't mad. If we were still living with Mother she would have told him to beat me with "The Enforcer," that board they used. He only hit us under her direction with

Chapter 2: Shelter from the Storm

very few exceptions. He didn't like hitting us. She told him to "spank" me once so he grabbed "The Enforcer" and shut my bedroom door. He looked at me and with a smile said "Scream like your dying" as he beat the hell out of my bed. When he left my room he said "Stay in here until those tears dry up." That way Mother wouldn't see I wasn't crying. That was so cool.

Debbie Geiger and I were voted Wittiest of 1970

Instead of getting mad at me for drinking, Dad threw me a party. He said that since I was a man now he wanted me to meet some of his friends. The night of the party he started off by putting a jigger of bourbon in my coke, but by the end of the night he was putting a jigger of coke in my bourbon.

I had the diction and motor skills of Dudley Moore in Arthur. I also thought I was as hysterically funny as he was. I told you I had the ability to amuse myself, right? When I realized that I was the only one that was laughing, I went to my room.

I struggled to get my clothes off. I was wearing a sweatshirt that seemed to be fighting as hard to stay on as I was to get it off. I started twirling around and knocked the lamp off the dresser. It was dark now and I was still fighting with my clothes. I was hopping around on one foot trying to get my pants off but couldn't get my foot freed from my pant leg. As I fell back on my bed, I realized I still had my shoes on.

I finally won the fight with my clothes. I laid there trying to catch my breath. The bed began to spin. Slow at first and then faster and faster. I had been told by friends if this ever happened to put my foot on the floor and the spinning would stop. It didn't. Obviously the floor was spinning too.

There was a rumbling in my stomach and I knew it was about to erupt. I ran to the bathroom in my skivvies, hung my head in the toilet and watched the food I had eaten all day reappear. Not only did it look bad, it didn't taste the same either. I couldn't remember the last time I ate corn? Why was that there? Does corn ever digest?

As my stomach drained into the toilet Dad walked up to the bathroom door with a couple of his buddies. They

Chapter 2: Shelter from the Storm

were laughing at how drunk I was. Dad was holding a green Tupperware glass and said "Here boy drink this." I was so drunk and showing everyone what a man I was I would drink anything at that point. I turned it up and drank half of it before I realized that it was warm salt water. It gave me the dry heaves. That's the last thing I remember about my party.

The next day I woke up with the worst headache of my young life and the taste of yesterday's garbage in my mouth. The smell of bourbon turned my stomach. Hell, the smell of any alcohol did. To me beer was like drinking the drug test, I hated it. I was done with drinking and it was eight years before I took another one.

This is a picture of Dad and Ronnie deep sea fishing in Florida. Dad was so proud of Ronnie for that catch. They bonded and I was flirting with two sisters from Nashville. I wish I had that time with Dad back.

He passed away on May 21, 1987, as hard as it was to accept, I was glad we had been so close the last fifteen years or so of his life. We hadn't always been as close as I would have liked.

After all these years I still think of him daily and strive to make him proud of me. It's important. It always has been. When I was growing up Dad always seemed to be a pretty straitlaced guy. He never really showed much of a sense of humor. But now as I look back there are glimpses of his humor. I think we were much more alike than I thought growing up.

It's funny; my mother always demanded respect and never got it. Dad had it without asking for it. He earned it every day.

As I said my dad wasn't an educated man, but he was a very smart man. He knew if he told me not to drink that I would just do it behind his back. By making me sick he knew for sure I wouldn't drink anymore.

I believe he saved my life that night. I watched a lot of my friends get mangled and even killed in DUI accidents as the years went by. I could have been one of them, but I didn't drink.

Thank God for marijuana!

Chapter Three:
You've Got a Friend

A lot of people have told me after hearing about how my mother treated me that they're surprised that I don't hate all women. She is one woman. Granted she is mean as hell and self-centered but I knew even as a child she was different from other mothers.

As a kid my best friends were always girls. I loved them, I was drawn to them. In the first grade my best friend was Debby Oakley. We talked and played together at recess. The teacher thought that was strange and read a little too much into it. She made the boys play on one side of the basketball court and the girls on the other. Debby and I met at half court. We took the same school bus home and sometimes would talk right through our stops and our parents would have to come to school to pick us up.

I could talk to her about anything. That was why I liked girls as friends so much because you could pour your heart out to them and they never judged you. Debby would listen and offer advice on anything I wanted to talk about. She was the first of many friends that just happened to be female. After the first grade I moved and went to another school but Debby and I went to the same high school and again we were the best of friends, as we are today. I have known Debby longer than anyone except my family. We have helped each other through many of life's crisis. She helped define how I saw and treated the opposite sex.

The person who had the most influence on how I saw other females was Bea. I met her when I was in the sixth grade. We were both members of the Safety Patrol and met at a movie theater. The school would treat the safety patrol kids to a movie once a year. That was better than paying us I guess. There was a kid named Mark sitting next to her at the movie and she said "Hey get up and let Mitch sit there, he's cute." That started our friendship. She was my girlfriend from the sixth to the eighth grade. But we remained best friends until we graduated.

Bea was beautiful. She had dark brown hair, Brown eyes, a great tan and a beautiful warm smile with perfect teeth. She reminded me a lot of Marlo Thomas from the TV Series *That Girl*. That show came on when we were in high school. She was always happy and bubbly like Ann Marie, the character Marlo played. She was a "good girl" almost to a fault. She was the kind of girl you would be proud to introduce to your parents. But I tried to keep her away from my mother, she could turn bubbly to bummed in one visit.

When Bea decided she just wanted to be friends in the eighth grade it kind of surprised me. I had talked to her on the phone every night for two years. She was my escape from what was going on at home. She was like family to me. I told her everything. But the phone calls every night didn't stop. She had other boyfriends but it didn't affect our friendship.

She also told me everything about her including what

Chapter 3: You've Got a Friend

she liked and how she liked to be treated. She liked to have the door opened for her. She liked being treated like a lady and didn't like it if you cussed around her. She was a lady in every sense of the word. I was in daily contact with her for six years so I learned how to treat girls with respect. She taught me how to love. Not like a man loves a woman but how you love another person, with respect and understanding. A wholesome kind of love, she would feel right at home on Walton's mountain.

I don't know that I was ever in love with her but I definitely loved her and she loved me. I found that as her friend I got to do everything her boyfriend got to do because she was such a good girl. The only major difference was the boyfriends were short term and I was long term.

We went downtown together, to movies, out to eat and to each other's house. I always saw us getting back together at some point but that never happened. We came close a few times but she was afraid it would ruin our friendship. It would have been worth the gamble for me. I didn't think anything would ever come between us.

Bea was the best friend I ever had. She truly cared if I was happy or sad. If I was sad she would do whatever it took to make me laugh and get into a better mood before she would let me get off the phone.

Radio Daze

Chapter 3: You've Got a Friend

She lived around the corner from me and many times when I was pissed off about something going on at home I would go to Bea's and she would give me a hug, hold my hand and talk to me until things were better.

She was very close to her mom and told her a lot about me and what my family was like. Her family was so close and loving, a lot different from my family. When her mom heard that my parents were divorcing she wanted to adopt me and she wasn't kidding. She talked to me about it for months.

Bea wasn't just a good girl, she was a good person. In fact she was the best person I have ever known. She cared more about me than anyone ever has. She showed me what love was. It didn't have to be about being my girlfriend, just caring. I don't know what I would have done if it hadn't been for her. I know that God brought her into my life to show me that I was loved. To help guide me through the hard times at home. She is the reason I don't hate women. That I respect them and love them, she showed me not only what love is but how to express it. She told me love is about giving. She taught me that if you really love someone, their happiness and desires are more important than your own. To never offer your heart to someone who isn't willing to do the same. If they are willing to put their heart in your hand, only then are they worthy of yours. If you want trust, you must first give trust. A relationship is about giving, not taking, expressing love not suppressing it.

What I learned from Bea has stayed with me all my life. It was easy for her to express how she felt, what was in her heart. From the time I spent with her, I learned to do the same. That was the greatest gift anyone has ever given me.

Chapter Four:
Teacher

The first time I met John Hester I was in the 7th grade. Frayser was a combination Junior/Senior High School. My homeroom teacher was a young, beautiful, somewhat strict lady named Mrs. Lundsford. She taught 7th Grade Art. Right across the hall was Mr. Hester who was in his mid thirties, which was really old at the time. He taught Senior English and Drama. He was a bit intimidating just by the mere fact that he was a senior high teacher and a bit condescending to the junior high students.

I was sitting outside my homeroom on a white domed trash can before school started one morning with a sizeable crowd standing around me. I was doing what I love to do, entertaining. I was telling jokes and stories. It was kind of my job as the class clown; I loved to make people laugh.

Mr. Hester was walking to his classroom. He reached through the group of students, tugged on my sleeve and said "C'mon, let's ride horsey together." If he didn't have two trash cans in his room, I knew I was in trouble. Again.

He took me into his classroom and started writing out a detention slip. As he handed it to me he asked "Do you know who I am?" I looked at the signature on the slip and said "I'm guessing John Hester." He tried not to laugh but I got a little one out of him as he asked "But do you know who else I am?" After an uncomfortable pause of silence he continued "I play organ at your church." I asked him to turn around and looked at the back of his head. He played with his back to the congregation and had a little white patch that stood out against a full head of brown hair. "You sure do!" I said as I recognized the back of his head.

He had seen me enough at church to know that I was outgoing, enjoyed being the center of attention and making people laugh. As Shakespeare once said "All the world is a stage" but in my case it was the classroom...every one of them. What Mr. Hester couldn't have known was that although my family was at Church every time the doors opened, we made The Bundy's look like the Huxtables.

I usually got to school before the doors opened because I left the house as early as possible and came home as late as I possibly could. Even detention was better than going home. As soon as I left my house a smile would creep across my face and it never left until I walked back in the door that afternoon. While laughter was my friend and constant companion at school, it was my enemy at home.

Mr. Hester told me that he was casting the Christmas play, *A Christmas Carol* and needed a junior high student to play Tiny Tim. "I'll tell you what" he said "I'll tear up this detention slip if you agree to try out for the part. You don't even have to get it, just try out for it." I agreed and low and behold I got the part.

Chapter 4: Teacher

Being on stage for the first time was the biggest rush I ever had. I loved it. When the play was over he asked me how I liked it, I couldn't stop talking about it. At the time, that was the highlight of my life. Acting gave me another place to escape. When I was studying my lines at home I could escape into the character and tune Mother out. Learning to tune my mother out was also good training for my future ex-wife.

Then he dropped the bomb. He had played me like a drum. He knew that being on the real stage would be so much better than just entertaining the classroom. He warned me that Drama was an elective and that he didn't have to let me take it. He said he wouldn't if I didn't maintain an S in conduct and nothing below a C in any subject for the next year and a half. "I don't mean a C average, I mean nothing below a C" making himself crystal clear. I realized that meant that all the class clown stuff had to be before and after school or between classes. It was tough but I did it, I had to. He turned my life around with that little deal because I knew I wanted to do more plays and that's what he was counting on.

When I finally got into Drama almost two years later, our first assignment was to do a sales speech. We could pick anything we wanted to sell. I thought long and hard before deciding on a frying pan. My mother had just bought a new Teflon pan. I grabbed the old one out of the trash and took the new one too. This was going to be great. I knew exactly what I was going to do.

Radio Daze

When I did my speech I called the new one a "Small State" pan and the old one was of course a Teflon pan. I said that they both had been used an equal number of times. "As you can see the Teflon pan is all scratched up, but the Small State pan looks brand new" (imagine that). I went on for the three minutes that I had to talk and concluded by saying "...so remember, you're in good pans with Small State." The class went wild with laughter, they never saw it coming. It couldn't have gone better. That was the first time I ever got a laugh in class without disturbing it. I did it by doing my assignment. Amazing.

The next day at the beginning of class Mr. Hester asked me to step out into the hall with him. I thought you have **got** to be kidding me. He's going to get onto me for using humor in my speech.

When I got outside Mr. Hester shut the door so the rest of the class couldn't hear what he was saying to me. "You know I videotaped the speeches yesterday right?" "Yes sir" I said waiting for him to scold me as only Hester could. But to my surprise he told me he had played my speech for the advanced students "and they agree with me in recommending that you pursue a career in broadcasting" he said with a big smile. In the 9th grade he saw that I could have a career in radio. I've enjoyed my profession now for over thirty years because of the insight of John Hester. I looked forward to going to work every day. I've enjoyed my life to the fullest because of this amazing man who enjoyed his profession as much as

Chapter 4: Teacher

I've enjoyed mine.

One of the highpoints of high school for me was playing Preacher Haggler in "Dark of the Moon." I remember my cue line for my first scene in the play was "Here comes Preacher Haggler." As I walked onto the stage the audience died laughing. It was a daytime performance so it was just for the student body. They were laughing at the thought of me playing a preacher. I didn't break character; I waited for the laughter to die down and then delivered my line. I had learned to do that from watching TV shows like Carol Brunette and All in the Family.

When the scene was over, I went backstage and to my surprise Mr. Hester was waiting there for me. Hester was NEVER backstage during a performance. He was always out front watching the performance as a member of the audience. He gave me such a hug I thought he was going to crush my skull. As he did, he whispered to me "I can't believe that you didn't break character." "Thank you my son" I said and got ready for my next scene. Hester wanted us to always stay in character backstage. He never gave praise unless you deserved it. I was thrilled that he thought I did.

There was one scene where I had to kneel down and talk to a man praying during the Brush Arbor (outdoor) Revival. During rehearsals I just pretended to be talking to him, but I got so much energy from what John had said I really was Preacher Haggler. I borrowed some lines from other parts of the play and spoke as if I was trying to get him to really accept Jesus. His name was Wayne Foropoulos and only he could hear me. He was supposed to stand, raise his hands over his head and proclaim "Halleluiah I'm saved, I'm saved." When he did tears were running down his face because of what I had said to him. That really gave me a shot of adrenalin. He was as into it as I was. He was a strong Christian and is now a preacher himself.

Then as other cast members circled me chanting, I had to preach above them. The louder I got, the more I got into being the preacher. It was one of the most memorable scenes I was ever in and I had been in *Tom Jones*, *Oliver*, *Dark of the Moon* and *Westside Story* among others.

I had the second male lead. My friend Ray Spain was the lead. As we did the curtain call I came out just before Ray and Patricia Cox (the female lead) to take my bow, when I did, the standing ovation started. I will remember that feeling for the rest of my life. Chills went up my back and every hair on my head felt like it was standing straight up. I never got praise for anything at home and the feeling of being appreciated was overwhelming for me. It brought tears to my eyes and joy to my heart. John Hester was responsible for that feeling. He saw years before that with his guidance and direction what I could achieve.

Later in the year our assignment was to interview an

Chapter 4: Teacher

influential person in Memphis. I chose the number one DJ in Memphis, George Klein. I hitchhiked from Frayser High School to 56 WHBQ, across town to do the interview.

I was sitting in the lobby. I was so excited I was "shaking like a leaf on a tree" to quote Elvis from "All Shook Up." It was as if it was Christmas morning. GK was the most famous DJ in town and had been for as long as I could remember. He had a TV show called Talent Party. It was Memphis' version of American Bandstand. Even if he didn't have all that going for him, it was a known fact that he was Elvis' best friend. He met Elvis in the eighth grade. He was the only one to be in the inner circle from then until the end, August 16, 1977.

I can't remember ever being that shaken. I was starting to wonder if I would be able to even do the interview. As I was thinking maybe I had made a mistake, the receptionist called my name and said "Mr. Klein is ready to see you now." As she walked me back to his office, I felt as if my feet weighted a ton. His office didn't look like I thought it would. It didn't look like an office at all. It was a long thin room with shelves of 45's and a desk pushed up against the wall.

As we entered the room, he was on the phone facing the wall. I heard that famous voice of his for the first time in person. She pointed to a chair and I sat down and waited for him to finish his phone call. When he did, he turned around in his chair. I got a lump in my throat and my mouth dried up. I wasn't sure I would even be able to speak. I was as scared to meet him as I would have been to meet Elvis himself. I knew this was as close as I would ever be to the king.

I expected him to be like any other adult talking to a kid. You know, acting superior, talking down to me and rushing me through the interview. This would be the first of many times George would surprise me with his kindness. He could see how star struck I was. He took control by asking "What's your last name?"

"McCracken"

"Are you related to Sonny McCracken?"

"Yes Sir, he's my cousin."

"Did you know he went to school with Elvis and me?"

"No Sir, I didn't."

George told me a few things about Sonny that I didn't know and it really relaxed me. I remember WHBQ playing one of Sonny's songs called "In the Middle of a Lonely, Lonely Night". I understood then how that happened. It wasn't a hit but George gave him a shot. I felt like I had known George all my life. The nerves were gone and I was just enjoying the time he allowed a high school student to spend with him.

Chapter 4: Teacher

I got so comfortable with him that I started opening up to him. He asked me "Of all the people in Memphis you could have interviewed, why did you choose me?" "To be honest" I said "because I want to be you when I grow up, well a DJ anyway." We laughed and then he invited me to come back anytime I wanted to use the production studios and he would help me perfect my delivery.

That was not an empty offer. I spent as much time at WHBQ as some of their employees. I would hitchhike to the station to do pretend air shifts called air checks. George would critique them for me. Years later, when the time came, he recommended me for my first radio job at WMC-FM100.

Knowing my career choice Mr. Hester was proud of my choice on that project. He was becoming a major influence in my life. When my parents were going through their divorce, John knew what I was going through. He knew I needed an adult in my life that believed in me. An adult to tell me everything was going to be okay and to keep me focused. He encouraged me and he wouldn't allow me to feel sorry for myself.

I stayed in touch with Mr. Hester over the years. I talked to him at least two or three times a year for over thirty years. I always wanted him to be proud of me. When I returned to Memphis in 1999 after 22 years on the National Radio Tour (I moved around a lot; New Orleans, LA, Las Vegas, etc), he was the first person that I had dinner with. I had a chance to tell him what an influence he had on my life and how much he meant to me.

Negative energy seems to be so much easier to share than positive. When someone has a positive effect on my life I try to make it a point to let them know. I thank God that I was given the chance to tell Mr. Hester what a wonderful teacher and human being he was and how he changed my life.

I used to daydream about getting up in front of the school and telling the student body what he meant to me, how he had made my life better. I never got a chance to do that, but I did get a chance to tell him. I guess everyone has a teacher that stands out in their life, John Hester was mine. He always believed in me, he saw something in me no one else did.

Mr. Hester recently passed away. As I look back at my life I see that Jesus put a lot of Christians around me to help me through the rough spots. John Hester was one of them. He will be missed. I will never forget what an influence he had on me. He was a great teacher, a great man and a true friend.

Chapter Five:
The End of Innocence

Right around the corner from the apartment I shared with my dad, lived a girl who was a couple of years younger than me. I knew she had a crush on me for the last couple of years. She was a cute little girl, kind of shy and whenever she got around me she would giggle a lot. She laughed at almost anything I said. Her name was Betsy. She was the last person that I ever thought would become a major player in my life, but she was going to change it forever.

I went walking down her street one day to see if I could find her. I was bored and wanted someone to talk to. She was close and I knew she would be willing. I was feeling lonely after my parents' divorce and she always made me feel good about myself because she gushed over me so much.

As I approached her house, there she was sitting on her front porch talking to her best friend Carol. I almost swallowed my tongue, she had grown a foot it seemed and was no longer the little girl that I felt so superior to.

She wasn't as skinny as before but certainly not overweight. Her hair style was different too. It had been short and wavy. The hair spray was also gone. It was longer with more of a natural look to it. Where before it didn't look like it would move in a hurricane, now it moved with just the slightest breeze, it was beautiful light brown with natural auburn highlights that glistened in the sunlight.

I hadn't seen her over the summer, it had just been a couple of months but she was a completely different person. As we talked I realized the silliness was also gone, it seemed she had turned into a totally natural earth mother. She had stopped dressing like a little school girl and had a new hip look. Not quite a hippie but very attractive. She was wearing Levi jeans and a midriff yellow halter top that looked great next to her flat tanned stomach. She was learning to play the acoustic guitar and was strumming on it as we talked. She had a beautiful round face with almond shaped eyes that were so sincere and trusting you could just get lost in them. They seemed to be all knowing and yet full of innocence at the same time. They smiled even when she didn't. She was so down to earth and in touch with who she was. She had an air of confidence that was missing before. You were just drawn to her. Her parents wouldn't let her wear makeup but she didn't need it. She had an olive complexion with just a slight touch of natural pink in her cheeks, so healthy looking with a smile that was contagious.

As the weeks went by I couldn't believe this was the same girl. Instead of dismissing her I couldn't get enough of her. I wanted to spend as much time with her as she would allow. I felt honored that she gave me as much attention as she did. I went from feeling superior to her to almost not worthy. She was no longer a little girl in my eyes she was now my peer in every way. She was only fourteen but seemed so much more mature. She was aware of the newfound respect I had for her and seemed

Chapter 5: The End of Innocence

to appreciate it. I was just afraid that she would make me fall for her and then dismiss me as I had her, to let me know how it felt. She showed me much more compassion than I had shown her when the tables were turned.

The year before, I had done an interview as a Drama class project with George Klein. He helped me with my air checks as he said he would. He let me do them in the production studios at WHBQ and I also did some on a little reel to reel tape machine in my bedroom.

One day I brought some of the tapes to Betsy's house to let her hear them. I wanted to see what she thought. Okay, I wanted to impress her. I trusted her to not make fun of me. Her opinion mattered more than anyone else's. She listened to them and told me how great I sounded. Even though I knew I didn't, it was good to hear that she thought so. She was my only friend that encouraged me in my quest of a radio career. The only one who believed in me at such an early stage. She made me believe I could really make it in radio.

Her parents were very protective of her. When I would go over to her house, her Mom would let her come out and talk to me but wouldn't allow me in the house. Every time I came over to see her, within minutes her little sister Molly would find a reason to come outside too. Seems her mom was sending her on a mission to keep an eye on us and make sure there was nothing going on.

Betsy and I had grown closer and closer over the last few months, she had become more than just a friend to me. But I wasn't sure how she felt. Although she was much more confident, she still wasn't the type of girl to come out and say how she felt.

She had a great climbing tree in her front yard, off to the side of the house. I came over to see her one day and we knew Molly would be coming out soon. She grabbed my hand and we ran to the tree and climbed it. There was one spot where two large limbs separated and we could both stand there. Molly looked everywhere for us but never thought to look up in the tree.

We were both laughing but not out loud so she wouldn't hear. She was almost right under us. She started calling Betsy's name and went around to the other side of the house. We had our chance and I gave Betsy a hug. I wanted to show her how much I cared about her. I had anticipated that hug for so long and now I finally got the chance. I can still feel the warmth of holding her body next to mine. I had grown so close to her. It felt so good to hold someone you cared for so much. The wind was blowing her hair in my face. Whatever shampoo she used smelled great, so fresh and clean with just a hint of honeysuckle.

As we pulled back I looked into her eyes and could see that the hug meant as much to her as it did to me. Those beautiful brown eyes told me for the first time it was okay to kiss her. I gave her our first kiss. I think it

Chapter 5: The End of Innocence

was her first kiss ever. It was so soft and tender. It told her how much she meant to me. It was like no other kiss. It had emotion and it gave me a bond with her that I had never felt before. I had kissed other girls but that was when we set out to meet somewhere for just that purpose. This was spontaneous. It was the first time it felt so natural, so caring and loving.

We started laughing out loud because it was such a tender moment and we were up in a tree. Just then Molly came around the house and looked up when she heard us. It was too late, we already had our moment. She had failed her mission.

Betsy was no longer the shy little girl that had been underfoot the year before. She had grown into a beautiful person both physically and spiritually and now she had my full attention. After that day her Mom would let me come into the house so she could keep an eye on us. Maybe a neighbor had seen us "up in a tree K-I-S-S-I-N-G."

When I played my tapes in the house her mom was even impressed and I started getting close to her as well. I would talk to her mom about how much I respected her family and about the breakup of mine. I think she saw how sincere I was. She started to see I was not just some kid who wanted to steal her daughter away, but someone that truly cared about her. Her dad still kept me at arm's length, but even he would warm up to me in time.

Like me, Betsy started taking Drama. My ego let me think she was trying to impress me although it was unnecessary. I couldn't be more impressed. She was my first true girlfriend. She was all I could think about. At night I went to sleep thinking about her and in the morning I couldn't wait to get to school to see her.

I changed my mind about why she took Drama when she got the lead in *Our Town*. I was also wrong about thinking I couldn't be more impressed. She blew me away. She was an actress and a damn good one. The play was all about understanding death. Betsy's character, Emily dies in the play. Just the thought of something like that happening to Betsy brought tears to my eyes and a lump in my throat. That was something I didn't want to think about. Life was so beautiful and happy for me then. For the first time it seemed I had found the right person for me. She was so warm and caring and I could talk to her about anything.

We decided to go to some speech tournaments together and compete in duet acting. We chose a piece from *The Apple Tree*, a trilogy of plays. We decided on *The Diary of Adam and Eve* by Mark Twain. In most cases you would just take a ten to twelve minute piece from a play and perform it straight through. But instead we took a few lines from several parts of the play and told the whole story of Adam and Eve. We went from Adam's pain in the side which of course was Eve's arrival, to naming the animals, having kids and finally being banned by God from the Garden of Eden.

Chapter 5: The End of Innocence

Betsy delivered her lines with a combination of innocence and wisdom that Eve herself must have had, she was flawless in her portrayal of Eve. We placed almost everywhere we competed but only second or third place, first place always seemed to elude us.

Betsy Reno

We were a couple now and things couldn't be much better. Betsy made up for all the unhappiness at home. When things were bad at home all I had to do is think about her and nothing else seemed to matter. She was my oasis in the desert. As good as things were with us, you have to remember that we were teenagers and the only thing constant with teens is change.

Other guys at school were seeing the change in her too. She was getting a lot more attention from the male population and I guess she was wondering if she should test the waters with some of them. We started to drift apart as she became interested in some of the other guys at school. One in particular that also played guitar.

She wanted to explore what else was out there. I couldn't get mad because that would drive her away from me. Her father was an angry man and she told me on many occasions that one of the things she liked best about me was that I was always funny and upbeat, that I never lost my temper. So I had to be satisfied with my new role as friend and not boyfriend. But she did make me promise that when she turned sixteen I would take her out on her first date and I looked forward to that. It gave me hope.

Everyone was seeing what a different person she was and she was enjoying it. I couldn't and wouldn't take that away from her. I looked at our relationship as long term so I knew I had to be patient. I was sure that in time she would realize that we were supposed to be together. Don't all true romantics think that?

While she moved on I still cared very much for her. She had become the most important person in my life. I couldn't just forget that as if it never happened. Or how much she believed in me and encouraged me, I needed that. My mother was so negative towards me and destroyed my self-esteem. That's why Betsy's belief in me meant so much. I wasn't used to hearing that. She didn't realize that the class clowns, the funny guys were usually more insecure than most. I know I was. She did know how good it made me feel to hear praise and she made me feel good a lot. We remained close friends and could still talk about anything.

By the time her birthday rolled around I had just bought her family car from her dad. He and I had become closer after Betsy told him I was no longer her boyfriend. He had no idea what we had planned for that car. He did give me a great deal on it: the car, five tires and five hubcaps for just ninety bucks. It was a ten year

Chapter 5: The End of Innocence

old Oldsmobile 98, the five hubcaps? One was to a Chevy, one to a Ford, two to a Pontiac and never could decide what the other one went to but none of them would fit my new car. Oh, and about the tires that came with it? None of them had any tread. They were as bald as he was.

She thought it was so strange going out with me in her car, although she did seem to be comfortable enough to put her feet up on my dashboard. I was a bit nervous about going out with her. My feelings for her hadn't changed. If anything, they had grown stronger. I hadn't been interested in anybody else. I was just waiting for this date to see where, if anywhere, it might lead. I knew she had been interested in several other guys but I didn't know if she was serious with any of them. She didn't say and I didn't ask.

George Klein

Through my friendship with George Klein, I had become friends with several DJ's at WHBQ. One of them was Robert W. Walker who was one of the coolest DJ's at the time. He did the 6-9 pm air shift right after George. He had the most low key deliveries of any of the AM Radio jocks. Everything seemed to just roll of his tongue. He could make the honor society's big chess game sound cool.

Betsy and I were going to meet Rob and his girlfriend at a station promotion. It was some kind of crafts show at the Mid South Coliseum and she seemed to be pretty impressed with that. When we got together for this date it was like we had never been apart. She was still easy to talk to, still comfortable to be around and we got a lot closer that night. I started to feel the bond that I had first felt in her tree so long ago.

With her birthday came new freedoms like perfume, I don't know what it was but it sure was calling my name. I bought her a lot of little trinkets like glass blown flowers, little stuffed animals, incense, etc. She was thrilled. I guess it was the first time a guy bought anything for her. She was jumping up and down with excitement and she had a beautiful smile on her face. If Oprah's couch was around then, I'm sure she would have found it. That, along with the scent of her new perfume was getting to me. I was like the cat in the cartoons that floats through the air smelling the scent of the fish. It was all I could do to refrain from kissing her. She gave me that go ahead look that she had given me so many times before but I was afraid to move too fast, I didn't want to blow it with her.

The thing she had always liked about me was my ability to make people laugh. I seemed fearless to her. She saw me as a confident guy who never doubted himself. I knew right then I shouldn't let that opportunity

Chapter 5: The End of Innocence

slip by. It looked to me as if we were going to get back together and I wanted that more than anything.

As I drove her home I told her that I almost kissed her earlier at the craft show. A smirk and then a smile slowly crept across her face as she said "I know, I could tell." I was just pulling up to the side of her house where her parents couldn't see us. I said "would that be okay, if I kissed you?" In her shy way she just looked down and shook her head yes. I had dreamed of this moment since we had stopped seeing each other. I gave her a passionate kiss and then another and another, my heart was about to jump out of my chest. Then she stopped me.

"I could stay out here with you all night but my parents will be looking for me." She got out and asked me not to walk her to the door because she didn't want to deal with her parents. I think she knew I would want to kiss her goodnight at the door and the only reason her parents let her go with me is because they thought we were just friends now.

I waited until she walked in the house and drove home with a big grin on my face. Now I knew we were getting back together. I savored those words she said to me, "I could stay out here with you all night." When we talked the next day she asked me not to tell anyone what happened the night before. She had to take care of a few things before we could let people know we were getting back together. Was she seeing someone else? I didn't care, I couldn't be happier. Things were going so well with Betsy and me. There were no jealously issues, I knew she cared about me for a couple of years before we got together and she felt like I finally saw her for the person she was. We were always laughing, holding hands and hugging. It was like that song by The Turtles called "Happy Together," that we were.

Betsy went to Nashville to a speech tournament where she competed in debate. She was supposed to be back home Saturday night. Sunday afternoon we were going to get together and work on *The Diary of Adam and Eve*. I had made some changes to hopefully do better in the next speech tournament.

I was waiting for her phone call but when it came it wasn't Betsy. It was Carol, her best friend, telling me that Betsy was dead. I went into shock. I could feel my eyes well up with tears. My mouth dried up and I got a lump in my throat. I felt my knees begin to buckle. I was devastated. How could this be? How could God let this happen? How could she be gone so quickly, with no warning?

Through her tears Carol told me there had been a terrible accident on the way home from Nashville the night before. It seems that the driver of the car Betsy was in fell asleep at the wheel. He drifted into some gravel on the shoulder of the road. Instead of easing back onto the highway he was startled and jerked the wheel. The car flipped over several times and three girls had been killed.

Chapter 5: The End of Innocence

Betsy was thrown from the car and landed on her cheek snapping her neck, she died instantly.

I couldn't believe that I would never talk to her again. Never hold her or kiss her. She was gone forever. I felt my whole world had just come to an end.

The driver survived along with another passenger. For a year I plotted his death. I came up with several different scenarios, each one more painful than the last. In time I realized it was an accident and that he would have to live with that for the rest of his life. When you are hurt like that you have to blame someone. I blamed him.

I walked around in a daze for what seemed like a lifetime until the day before her funeral. At about two in the morning, I found myself in that tree in Betsy's front yard where we had shared our first kiss. It was so dark and quiet yet I could still hear that infectious laugh of hers. I looked over at her bedroom window and of course the light was out, it was not just a bad dream.

I sat where we had stood that day. I leaned back and looked up into the sky. It was a clear night. You could see every star in the sky. As I stared into space I thought if only she hadn't gone to Nashville. If only she had rode in another car. If only he hadn't fallen asleep. There were a hundred "if onlys," I wanted my time with her back so badly so I could savor every moment of it.

Radio Daze

I cried for hours. I loved her with all my heart and never had the chance to tell her. Three little words that seemed so hard to say would be so easy now. It didn't matter if she felt the same for me as I thought it would. I needed her to know how much she meant to me. How comfortable I was with her. How much it meant to me that she believed in me.

When things were bad at home she could always make me feel better, yet I never told her that. So many feelings not expressed. Did she know? Could she feel how much I cared about her? If she could see I wanted to kiss her, couldn't she see how much I loved her? Surely she did. I had to believe she did. That was the end of innocence for me. I understood that tragedy wasn't just something that happened to other people. It happened to me in a big way.

Attending her funeral would prove to be one of the most difficult things I ever did. A group of her close friends stayed with her all night before the funeral. It was to be a closed casket service but her older sister Amy wanted to say goodbye as we all did. She opened the casket that night. As she stood there looking down at her little sister she locked her knees. She was wearing one of those one piece dresses that I had seen Betsy wear so many times. She had the same long brown hair. Betsy stood with her knees locked like that. I thought for a moment it was Betsy standing there. It was all I could do to not call out her name. No one knew how close we had become since her birthday. I was calm on the outside but

Chapter 5: The End of Innocence

I was screaming on the inside. The pain was unbearable.

We gave Amy a few minutes alone with her and then slowly walked up to the casket. When I looked down at her it was as if she were sleeping. She had a single cut on her index finger of her right hand and a few scratches on her cheek. They were the only visible injuries. She looked so beautiful. I couldn't believe she was gone. I wanted to stroke her hair, touch her hand or even kiss her to say goodbye. But I remembered what my dad said. He at one time had been an embalmer. He told me that no matter how natural a person looks, they don't feel the same and never touch them. He said to remember what she was like when she was alive. It was so hard to resist but for once I listened to what the old man said and I'm glad I did. Nothing was going to replace the memory of that first tender kiss, the night of her sixteenth birthday and all the laughs and tender moments we had shared. In hindsight I guess I did tell her that I loved her, just not in so many words.

There were probably thirty people in the cathedral at the funeral home that night and we were all scattered around having our individual conversations when a hush suddenly came over the room. Every one of us simultaneously felt Betsy's presence. There was a moment of silence as we all took in the unmistakable feeling of Betsy being there with us enjoying the love for her that was in the room that night. It was just for a moment and she was gone. We all started talking again but it was about the feeling we all had just shared.

Later that day at the funeral it seemed the whole school turned out. She had touched so many lives with her kindness and understanding. So many friends, I guess they loved her too. Maybe she made everyone feel as loved and appreciated as she made me feel. Every one of us that had stayed the night with her got a single long stem red rose. At the end of the service one by one we filed by, kissed the rose and placed it on top of the casket. It was a loving gesture and a final goodbye to a beautiful soul.

Betsy and I had signed up for several more tournaments so I picked another partner and continued doing the cutting. I knew it wasn't going to be easy doing it without Betsy. In fact I wasn't sure I could, but I wanted to try.

The first performance was really going well until my last speech. For the first time the words seemed to come to life. They weren't just words. They had real meaning to me now. Adam and Eve had been banned from the Garden of Eden. Adam was on his knees watering a little flower garden.

My Drama teacher, Mr. Hester taught me that when I was on stage or performing to look just over the head of the audience and they would feel as if I was looking into their eyes. This time I looked out into the audience making deliberate eye contact with each and every one of them. I wanted them to feel the pain I was feeling. The same pain that Adam must have experienced, I felt cheated by God as I'm sure Adam did.

I stopped watering and leaned back on my haunches. I struggled to hold back the tears as I looked out at the audience so they could see the pain in my face even before I spoke. With a weak and shaky voice I delivered my lines "I was mistaken about Eve. I thought she talked too much. Eve died today, at first I thought it was a terrible tragedy when Eve and I had to leave the garden." My bottom lip began to quiver as tears began to stream down my face, it was one of the hardest things I've ever done. Somehow I found the strength to continue "...but now I know that wherever Eve was; there was Eden."

I dropped my head and began to cry for a moment before I regained my composure. As I said those words all I could think about was my beautiful Betsy and how every moment I spent with her was like a day in paradise. I wasn't acting, I was grieving.

The small audience of twenty to twenty five sat silently until I got it together enough to rise from my knees and then broke into applause. We took first place almost everywhere we performed after the accident and yet I felt guilty. As if I was taking advantage of the situation. I thought I was dishonoring Betsy's memory. Mr. Hester told me that's what actors do. They borrow from their life experiences to pull up the emotions they need for a part. He thought Betsy would be proud of me for continuing what we started together.

Radio Daze

Each performance after that was dedicated to her memory but I never told the audience that. I wanted to be judged on my performance and not on the pain I had to endure to deliver it. Through the pain, the memory of Betsy still brought joy to my heart. Eventually I was able to focus on that joy as I continued my search for a job in radio. She believed so strongly that I could make it as a DJ and I didn't want to let her down. I could have given up and felt sorry for myself but I knew what she expected of me. She respected me because I worked so hard at reaching my goal in broadcasting, it's amazing what we can achieve when someone we love believes in us.

Ironically, in a way, it was Betsy that indirectly got me my first job in radio. I was a senior and at the end of that school year I was the emcee of the Junior/Senior Banquet. The theme was "United We Stand" from the song by The Brotherhood of Man.

In the chow line at the banquet

Someone lost a long white glove. I had to go up on stage to make the announcement and try to find the owner. As I walked up the stairs to the stage I looked at the back wall as the lights came up. I saw the words UNITED WE STAND spelled out in giant letters. It occurred to me that until the accident when you entered the school lobby there were so

Chapter 5: The End of Innocence

many groups of people. Jocks here, ROTC there, the Honor Society in another spot, but since the death of Betsy and the other two girls, the groups had disappeared as we all came together. We realized how precious life is and how quickly it can be taken away.

No one had said anything in public about the accident. As I looked out at all the couples out there, some of whom would be married within the next couple of years, I decided that I was going to put an end the silence that night.

When I reached the microphone I said "United We Stand means more to us here at Frayser than just a song on the radio. Have you noticed since the death this year of three of our friends, the groups have disappeared? We are all coming together to help each other through the tragedy that we have all had to deal with. The sad thing is next year when we come back to school the groups will reappear as the memory of how hurt we are starts to fade. Please don't let that happen. Remember you only get out of life what you put into it. Show the appreciation you have now for each other every day. You never know who you may lose tomorrow. Did someone lose this glove?" I got a standing ovation for that speech led by my friend Steve Weber.

A few days earlier I met with the Operations Manager of WMC (FM100) after getting a recommendation from George Klein. He was considering me for my first job in radio. His name was Bob Weber. That's right, Steve's father. When Steve told his dad what I did and how much it touched him, along with the recommendation...I got the job.

When he hired me, Mr. Weber said "We like to hire good people here at WMC. You are a good person Mitch" then with a chuckle he added "and some day you may be a good disc jockey too." It was then that I realized even with George's recommendation, without that speech I may have been passed over for the job because of my lack of experience. Betsy, who in life believed in me so much, turned out to be the one who made it happen. I still think of her often and wonder what life would be like had she not died.

Years later I ran into her sister Amy at Memphis in May. We talked on the phone a few times and went out to dinner once. I was thrilled to finally have a connection to Betsy again after all these years. I was just a kid at the time and yet my feelings for her never changed. I loved her as much as a child as I ever loved anyone in my adult life. I wanted to make that clear to Amy. It was as if I was reaching beyond the grave and expressing what I failed to say before the accident. All I could talk to Amy about was Betsy. I decided that wasn't fair to her. After all, she had moved on years ago. We drifted apart once again and went our separate ways. If I couldn't tell Betsy how much she meant to me all those years ago, at least I could tell Amy.

If ever there was a life interrupted, it was the young life of Betsy Reno.

Chapter Six:
Tell Her About It

One of the reasons I decided to become a DJ was because of my love of music and lack of talent. That's why I set my eyes on the coolest station in town, FM100. WMC was the third FM station in the country to go rock back in 1967. It was an Album Rock station that had very little structure as far as the format goes. It was as close to being a free form format station as you could get. I called the program director, Mike Powell at least once a week to find out if there were any openings.

In the meantime I was still doing my emcee thing in high school doing everything from assemblies to talent shows. If an emcee was needed for anything, I was ready and more than willing. Some of my friends thought I was an egomaniac, but it wasn't about that. Every time I got in front of a crowd with a microphone in my hand I would get a rush of adrenalin. I was scared but at the same time it was exciting. I always feared I would say something that I thought was funny and no one would laugh or that I would mispronounce someone's name, stutter or stammer, any of those things.

I remember once I said something that I thought was funny at a school assembly and only one person laughed. That was very uncomfortable. I didn't know what to do but I always thought fast on my feet, so I just said "Thanks Mom." As I looked in the direction of the laugh to see who it was, I lost it. "Oh my God," I said "it was my Mother," with that the whole auditorium broke into laughter.

That's why I enjoyed it so much, it was performing. I tried to get the audience to laugh and yet be personable and real at the same time. That's a hard line to walk. When you break that barrier between talking at an audience and talking to them, it's a great feeling.

It was my senior year and it was a big one for me. I was voted wittiest by my classmates, the runner up in the ugly man contest and voted Queen of the Powder puff. That's when the girls played tag football and some of the guys would dress in drag and act as the cheerleaders. I was also the Master of Ceremonies at the Junior/Senior Banquet.

I was really missing Betsy. I knew she would be so proud of me for what I was doing. I had gone out with a few girls, but they all paled in comparison. Betsy and I never fought. We were always laughing and having a good time. I just couldn't find that with anybody else. I needed someone I could share my hopes and dreams with but Betsy was the only one that seemed to be interested and she was gone. Thankfully that was about to change.

Just when you give up on ever finding another girl she walks into your life. I have always said you should never look for someone new. Because if you look, you never find, you just settle for whoever comes along. But you do have to keep your eyes open or she will walk in and out again before you ever know it.

Chapter 6: Tell Her About It

My eyes were wide open when Marty walked into my life. Did I say walked in? It was more like she stormed in. Marty and her friend Bev both came into my life like gangbusters. It happened so quickly that I don't remember where we met. The more I was around Marty the more I wanted to be around her. She was like Betsy in so many ways. It wasn't that she reminded of Betsy, she didn't. But the same things that I loved about Betsy were also there in Marty. Any girl I was with after Betsy was just a featured player in my life. But Marty was about to become a costar.

She was one of the most beautiful girls I've ever seen. She had long straight light brown hair, like Jane Asher (onetime girlfriend of Paul McCartney) and other models of the time. She had brown eyes that always seemed to have a light reflecting in them. They always had a gleam to them. Her lips were perfectly shaped, thin with that sexy little "M" shape on her top lip. Not too pronounced, very subtle but very beautiful and they seemed to scream at me "Kiss me, kiss me," man did I want to from the first day I met her.

Marty Clark

She struck me as an earth mother type like Betsy was. She had an air of confidence that made her even more attractive. Her smile was angelic and it was a sincere one, never forced. She had such a sweet soul I just wanted to make her smile and laugh as much as possible.

She was like "Cool chick Barbie." She was one those girls that looked great in whatever she wore. She could carry off wearing anything. Sometimes she wore short baby doll dresses that showed off her legs, but she also looked good in jeans and a t-shirt. No matter what she wore, she always looked great. Bev was the perfect best friend to Marty. She was also beautiful and as cool as Marty was.

I remember riding in the back seat of Marty's VW bug as we drove around and then parked in a church parking lot to smoke some hash while listening to an 8 track tape of Three Dog Night's *Suitable for Framing*. I was taking a hit from the pipe as Marty and Bev were talking. I tuned them out as I was looking at Marty. I was dumbfounded by her beauty. "Easy to be Hard" was playing and I couldn't help but fantasize about her as I listened to that song, In addition to the title the lyrics also got to me. "*How about a needing friend? I need a friend.*" We knew each other but I wanted to be more to her. Betsy was my best friend and Marty was the first one I thought I could get that close to since Betsy. I had never had a relationship with anyone that wasn't my friend first. I needed her to be that close to me. I was watching her as she talked and laughed with Bev. I just wanted to have her full attention for just a few minutes and try to make some ground, to see if there was anything there. I needed to know if the feeling was mutual or if I was getting in over my head.

Chapter 6: Tell Her About It

Marty quickly became not only my friend but indeed my best friend. We could talk about anything and we did. The best thing about my new best friend was she had a face that just mesmerized me. I could look into it for hours and never grow tired of it, just studying that smooth complexion. She had a perpetual smile and legs to die for. They were like her lips, perfectly shaped. I loved everything about her. I just wanted to hold her forever. This was the first time I really wanted to be with anyone since Betsy died and I wanted it so badly.

Marty was so much fun and what an audience she was. She had a quick wit so she got all my jokes. She liked to laugh as much as I did. For the first time in a long time I was completely content and happy. Marty and I got along so well and were having so much fun. We were just hanging out and riding around in her car with Bev, but I knew we had to move forward or there would be no relationship. That meant going out on dates and I had no job.

I was young and in my eyes I was invincible. I went to a department store (JB Hunters, I think) and picked out something like fifty-five albums. I took them into the men's bathroom. I went into a stall and removed the cellophane wrapping and the shuck around the album. Then I walked them back into the record department.

I found a salesman and said "Hey, I bought these with my income tax returns but my mom says I have to return them."

The salesman looked at how many I had and asked "You got a receipt?"

"No sir, I wasn't planning on returning them."

"Take your albums and get out of here."

"But my mom said…."

"Get out or I'll have security escort you out."

So I left with fifty-five brand new albums that I sold for two dollars each. By the weekend I had over a hundred dollars to take Marty out to the movies or wherever she wanted to go. That was a lot of money back then. It would last me a couple of months if I just spent it on dates and that's what I was planning on. I did keep a few for myself including the *Suitable for Framing* album, anytime I heard a song from it, it reminded me of Marty. I kept it for years.

We went out to movies and to hear different bands from Frayser and Bartlett. It didn't matter what we did we always had a good time. She had her bug but I didn't have a car. I couldn't believe she wouldn't let me drive hers. After all I had my driver's license.

One night Marty and I went out. When she drove me back home, I just sat there in the front seat. She had to beat her curfew home but I wouldn't get out. I made her come around and open the door for me and then walk

Chapter 6: Tell Her About It

me to the door. When we got there I looked at my feet and slightly swayed back and forth, while looking down as I said "Well, I had a good time." I slowly looked up at her. She was looking right through me as if to say "If you think I'm going to kiss you, you're crazy."

We both started laughing, I reached out and pulled her close to me to give her a hug. We pulled back and looked into each other's eyes. I looked down at those inviting lips and answered their call. I gave her a tender loving kiss making sure she could feel the passion I felt for her. I gave her another hug and she was on her way back to the car. I watched every step she took. She was wearing a short skirt and her cute little butt made it sway with each step like a matador taunting an eager bull.

Even though I wasn't a DJ yet I was a teenager and music was a big part of my life. It seemed every song that came on the radio reminded me of Marty. I laid in bed that night thinking about her as I listened to FM100, the station I wanted to go to work for. "Something" by the Beatles was playing and the lyrics really grabbed me while I listened and thought of Marty. I could just see that big smile of hers as I listened. It was like George Harrison had written the song about Marty instead of his wife Patti. Like he knew her as well as I did and how she always knew just what to say and do to make my heart jump out of my chest. That was what was so cool about music back then. You could identify with something (pun intended) in almost every song.

The next song that came on continued the Marty theme. It was "You Have made Me So Very Happy" by Blood, Sweat and Tears. That perfectly described how I felt about her. I thought about her as I drifted off to sleep.

The loneliness and heartache that I felt when Betsy died was starting to subside because of my feelings for Marty. She was like a gift from God to help me find the happiness that I thought was gone forever.

Marty was everything to me, just the mention of her name would put a bounce in my step and a smile on my face. Never a cross word or drama of any kind. My relationship with her was so different from what I thought a relationship between a man and a woman would be based on what I witnessed at home.

As much as I cared for her I never told her. She didn't know she was the center of my universe or how happy she made me. I never told her about Betsy or how lonely I was when we met. I didn't tell her how beautiful she was or how much I cared about her. I thought it would jinx things. I wasn't sure how she felt about me and I didn't want to scare her away. She had become so important in my life that I just had to tell her about it. I remembered how I felt when Betsy died, how sorry I was that I never told her how I felt. I made up my mind that no matter how hard it was, I was going to tell Marty how I felt the next time we talked.

Chapter 6: Tell Her About It

I called her that afternoon and I knew exactly how I was going to say it. When she answered the phone she said "oh good I was just going to call you. I've decided to go steady with a guy I met at my graduation."

It was like I had just been shot in the heart but I didn't let her know how badly hearing those words hurt. I got off the phone and went to lie down on my bed. Maybe if I had followed through with my plan to tell her how I felt things would have been different, but I didn't.

The next day I was going to Blytheville, AR to dig up Indian relics for the museum there with a few friends. We went in two cars. I rode with Terry in his brand new 1970 Mustang.

We got out the equipment and as I started to probe, Terry turned on his car stereo just as Yogi and George got there. The Chairmen of The Board's "Give Me Just a Little More Time (and Our Love Will Truly Grow)" was on, I had to walk away from them so they wouldn't see my eyes all glassed over. I knew to get over Marty I was going to have to refocus things. I put all my effort into finding a job in radio. Maybe that would impress Marty enough to come crawling back to me. Did I mention I'm a romanticist?

Side one
1. "Feelin' Alright" – 3:39
2. "Lady Samantha" – 2:53
3. "Dreaming Isn't Good for You" – 2:16
4. "A Change Is Gonna Come" – 3:10
5. "Eli's Comin'" – 2:41

Side two
1. "Easy to Be Hard" – 3:11
2. "Ain't That a Lotta Love" – 2:16
3. "King Solomon's Mines" – 2:29
4. "Circle for a Landing" – 2:20
5. "Celebrate" – 3:13

Chapter Seven:
The Last DJ

Other than Marty dumping me, things were going pretty good. I had a job as an usher at the Frayser Three Theaters and had just been promoted to the manager. But I was still actively pursuing a job as a disc jockey, doing whatever I had to do to land that job at FM100. I had the recommendation of George Klein from WHBQ and one from the Operations Manager's son, Steve Weber. In addition to that I already had a Radio commercial on the air at WHBQ and FM100.

Cobb Theaters, the chain I worked for was running a movie called Klute starring Jane Fonda and Donald Sutherland. Knowing my interest in radio the City Manager, Dick Smith asked me to write a commercial for the movie. I wrote a thirty second commercial that had an air of mystery to it. The movie was about a murderer on the loose and he was going after prostitutes. I wanted the commercial to capture the suspense of the movie.

He liked what I wrote when I read it to him and took it to WHBQ to have it recorded. He didn't like any of the announcer's versions but he liked the way I read it with that air of mystery to it

"One girl is dead...another is missing..." but you had to read it slow to give it that suspenseful feel. Dick said that everyone at HBQ sounded like, as he called them "Race Horse" disc jockey's and were reading it way too fast as he imitated them to me "This is what they were doing Onegirlisdeadandanotherismissing ..." So Dick had me come in and record it.

I was at the door tearing the tickets in the lobby opening night. People were actually commenting on the commercial. It was so unusual at the time to not have the announcer talking so fast. Not only had it set the right mood for the movie but it's more natural delivery made it stand out on the air. I wanted to tell each one of them that I wrote and voiced the commercial but I didn't. I knew then this radio thing was really going to work out for me. I won an award for that commercial from Cobb Theaters and they used it in several other markets (cities) where Klute was showing in their theaters.

It was at that time that Bob Weber finally hired me to do Saturday afternoons. He told me it would be at least a couple of years before I was ready for a full time shift. That's cool I thought, at least I had my foot in the door and had a full time job at the movie theater.

My first air shift got off to bad start. The first song I played was "You Know What I Mean" by Lee Michaels, followed by "Signs," the Five Man Electrical Band song. I forgot to pot (turn) down the Lee Michaels album and it went into the next song as I talked over "Signs." I was

Chapter 7: The Last DJ

freaking out, I could feel my face turning red and it felt like little pins sticking me all over. Not a good first impression, but I regrouped and got Jimi Hendrix's "Purple Haze" on without a hitch.

This was the air staff when I was there (just before I joined): Ron Michaels, Greg Hamilton, David Day, Jon Scott and Mike Powell

Right at the end of the Hendrix song the phone rang, well actually the phone doesn't ring in the control room at a radio station, it just blinks. "Hello, FM100" I said for the first time. "Mitch, this is your mother" said the voice on the other end. Aw Jeezus I thought the absolute LAST voice I wanted to hear. "We're all listening to you over here at Sears and I would appreciate it if you would refrain from playing any more gay songs" she said in a somewhat stern voice. "What? That's Jimi Hendrix, "Purple Haze" I explained. It was the early 70's in the south and most folks (including my mother) had very little tolerance for an alternative lifestyle.

"I don't care who he is, he said "Excuse me while I kiss this guy."

"Kiss the sky Mother, not kiss this guy. The song is about drugs, it's not a gay song."

"Drugs are cool, but no more gay songs. You are embarrassing me."

"Sorry about that, I forgot what a big day today is for you. Can you critique me after I get off the air, I really have to go." I pushed a button on the phone and poof she was gone. Man that was a great feeling. Wouldn't that have come in handy a few years ago?

Within a month and just after high school I went full time, doing the overnight shift. We had over 2,000 albums in the control room. You would play a song from

Chapter 7: The Last DJ

one and then set it on the floor and it was done for the day (except for current albums). At midnight everything went back in. I did graveyards so the whole world was open to me every night. That was when being a disc jockey really rocked. You could tell who was on the air just by the music that was being played. As a DJ you were allowed to be as creative as you wanted to be. I still remember a few real good segues that I did, you couldn't tell where one song ended and the other began.

I would play The Doors "Riders on the Storm" and right at the end there's some tinkering on the piano as you hear the storm. The piano stops and there's a clap of thunder and the sound of rain starts to fade. As soon as I heard that clap of thunder I would hit Leon Russell's "A Song for You" on the other turntable which begins with piano and by the time the rain stopped, it was into the vocal. It was a very smooth segueway.

Another one I like was playing the Beatles Abby Road Medley up until it goes into "She Came in Through the Bathroom Window" and I would have Joe Cocker's version cued up on the other turntable and switch to his version without missing a beat, at the end of the Cocker song I would continue the Beatles medley.

I would also play Quicksilver's Messenger Service's"Fresh Air" part of the song's lyrics say "Have another hit" (a second of silence) "of fresh air" and I would open the mic and fill that second with inhaling as if I was taking a hit off a joint. That was fun radio. Now you have to hear the station call letters between every song.

I was emceeing a show at a club one night and another jock from FM100 was there. He told me that I was *somebody* now. I never saw it that way. I was the same guy as always, I still loved to make people laugh. I was in awe of not only the people I interviewed but the people I worked with. They were the guys I listened to in high school. The weird thing is I never used humor on the air. I would talk about who was on the album or track I was playing. Or sometimes I would talk about upcoming concerts and other things going on around town. But I never tried to be funny. There's nothing worse than attempted humor on the air.

This was such a cool job. Not only did I get to interview but actually get to know people that I had heard on the radio for years. On the air I had the freedom to play just about anything I wanted to. Back then the disc jockey really had control of the sound of the station when he was on the air. It was everything I had dreamed of since the 9th grade. Now I was living it and enjoying every minute of it.

After starting to work at FM100 I noticed some of my friend's attitude towards me began to change. I started getting free passes to movies and concerts and when I would go to a bar I was welcomed from the stage and got applause from the patrons. All of a sudden I was a "cool, hip" guy. I was used to being seen as funny, but hip? Not so much.

Chapter 7: The Last DJ

One time before work I went to Filler Burger, a burger joint where we all hung out. You know, back the car in and watch to see who was cruisin' through. I got out of my car and saw one of my friends who had just pulled up. I approached the right side of his car. We were talking over his friend in the passenger seat. I didn't know him. Mike said "It's so weird, we went to high school together and now I hear you on the radio when I wake up." I just laughed and pointed out "You must have a paper route if you are up early enough to hear me." The guy next to him asked "Who is that?" Mike smiled and said "Mitch McCracken." Before he could say anything else the guy jerked his head back around to me and said "Not THE Mitch McCracken." I honestly didn't know what to say to that. How do you answer a question like that? Was I THE Mitch McCracken? I just looked at him in shock and said "Well I'm the one on the radio, if that's what you mean." If he knew that I was only making sixty dollars a week I don't think I would be perceived as THE anything, except maybe broke.

Jon Scott was on 7-Midnight and was the coolest jock in town, I looked up to him. I wanted to be just like him someday. But nobody was as cool as Jon. He was in his late twenties or early thirties and my mentor. People in Memphis still talk about him to this day. All the segues I talked about earlier, he taught me how to do them. He would listen to me when he got home and call me up and say "Hey, you know what would sound really good after that?"

The coolest thing about him was that he never took himself too seriously. He loved to mess with me. On my first graveyard shift Jon took the microphone and pushed it down behind the control board. I sat there for twenty minutes and never missed it. When I turned the mic on and started talking. It sounded like I was in a big well. I turned up the headphones and then the mic but nothing helped.

Jon was in the announcer's booth next to the control room with the lights out. There was a window so you could see into one room from the other. That is, if the lights were on. Jon could talk into the mic in the announcer's booth and I could hear him in my headphones but it didn't go over the air. It was hard for

Chapter 7: The Last DJ

him to talk he was laughing so hard. He asked "where's your mic" and lost it. I just hit the record and went next door, threw the door open, turned on the light to find Jon and two record guys rolling on the floor. How hip was I now?

Another time Jon came in the control room when I was reading the news and with his lighter lit the page I was reading on fire and left. You never knew what he would do next. Once when I doing a break, the lights came on in the announcer's booth and Jon was in a chair with wheels on it passing by the window mooning me. A good jock should never lose it on the air no matter what's going on, I wasn't that good. I lost it again with the mic still on.

As much fun as Jon was, he was also hipper than James Dean and his knowledge of music was impressive to say the least, Jon was one of the greatest jocks to ever grace the air waves in Memphis. We have had our share of some really good ones too like Rick Dees, Scott Shannon, Robert W. Walker, Wink Martindale, Jay Cook, Bob McLain, etc. Jon rented an old mansion out on James Road in the suburb of Raleigh and a lot of the artists that came to town for a concert stayed there, well at least the cool ones did. The Groundhogs even wrote a song called "3744 James Rd" about Jon's house. Jon's St. Bernard was named McPhee after The Groundhogs Tony McPhee.

David Bowie came to town right after Hunky Dory

was released and I believe he stayed at Jon's with his wife Angie. That was back in his Baggy pants stage like on the cover of that album before his metamorphosis into Ziggy Stardust and other characters. I also remember Ian Lloyd of Stories who had hits with "Mammy Blue" and "Brother Louie" was staying at Jon's house and he was talking to me about being afraid he sounded too much like Rod Stewart. Stewart was just starting his hot streak having just released *Every Picture Tells a Story*, his first solo album and *A Wink Is As Good As A Nod To A Blind Horse* with The Faces. I didn't think he sounded that much like Stewart. He went on to sing on almost all of Foreigner's albums but was never credited as a member of the group. I became friends with a lot of the local Memphis musicians like David Fleischman, Tony Joe White, Keith Sykes, Sid Selvidge, Jack Holder, Tommy Cathey, Bill Gregory, Robert Johnson, Legendary Stax session guitarist Steve Cropper and his partner at TMI, Jerry Williams.

Even though I was young and doing the all night show I still got to sit in and interview some really big names at the time. Once Jon allowed me to observe but not talk when he interviewed Mountain guitarist Leslie West and bassist Felix Pappalardi, that was really a good interview. By good I mean informative. At the time "Mississippi Queen" was one of my favorite songs. The interview was mostly with Felix though talking about his days as Cream's producer. He was involved with getting Clapton signed to RSO Records.

Chapter 7: The Last DJ

Robert Stigwood wanted to sign the Bee Gees which Felix also handled and he told Stigwood that he would give him the Bee Gees BUT he would also have to take Eric Clapton. Stigwood didn't realize what he was getting according to Felix. While he was talking about that, Leslie West was smacking chicken into the other microphone. His mic was finally killed to end the noise.

Jon called me one night and told me that he was going to be interviewing George Harrison's father, Harry and to come in early if I wanted to sit in and watch. I got there about 10:30 or 11 as I recall. A few minutes later there was a ring at the back door (another light). Jon asked me to let them in and there stood Don Nix, a local artist and songwriter (the first to be signed to Leon Russell's Shelter Records) and Klaus Voorman along with a short elderly English gentleman who I'm guessing is Harry.

They talked for quite a while about the Concert for Bangladesh, the album and the movie. Don Nix was in the backup band on both.

Don's an excellent songwriter and wrote a killer song called "Going Down" that was originally recorded by a local Memphis group called Moloch. It was later recorded by Freddie King on Shelter and many more artists have also covered including Jeff Beck. Don also wrote a song recorded by Albert King on his **Love Joy** album that Don also produced called "Everybody Wants to Go to Heaven (But Nobody Wants to Die)." That's one of my favorite Don Nix songs. Don has had a great career, the next year he formed the Alabama State Troupers with other notable Memphis musicians like bluesman Furry Lewis, Brenda Patterson and Ken Woodley. Don was also a member of the Mar-Keys with his high school buddies Steve Cropper and Duck Dunn. Wayne Jackson of the Memphis Horns was also in the group. They had a hit with the instrumental "Last Night" on the Satellite Records label which later became Stax.

Harry told Jon that his house was the only one that would allow the group that would become the Beatles to practice there. They went by The Quarrymen and then changed their name to the Silver Beatles before The Beatles.

The most interesting thing to me that Harry said that night was off mic when he asked how we liked Clapton's playing in the movie. I said "Excellent as always." "Good, I'll let George know you thought so" he said with a strange look on his face. "What do mean" I asked. He told us "If you saw the movie, it put the spotlight on everyone from Leon Russell to Bob Dylan, Ringo Starr even Ravi Shankar but not Clapton." According to Harry, "that was because Clapton was so messed up that George had to go in and overdub everything Clapton had played. The only ones that heard Clapton were at the concert."

I knew that Clapton hadn't made any of the rehearsals except the final sound check. That was pretty well publicized. I was blown away. It came out years later that

Chapter 7: The Last DJ

Clapton had problems with drugs, heroin in particular. He is of course off drugs now and spends much of his time and money helping others kick drugs through his charitable organizations.

What's interesting about "While My Guitar Gently Weeps" is that when it was recorded by the Beatles on The White Album there was a big deal about Clapton playing lead guitar on a Beatles album. The Concert for Bangladesh was to be the first public performance of the song by Eric Clapton and now we know his work was overdubbed by George Harrison, who wrote it.

I also got to emcee some great shows at the Overton Park Shell in midtown like Procol Harem, Leon Russell and the Shelter People and Lee Michaels.

Wishbone Ash came to town and we did a live broadcast of a concert from Ardent Recording Studios. MCA Records released a promotional EP of that show. Those tracks are now on the Argus CD as bonus tracks.

In addition to my graveyard shift, I also did a Saturday 7 to midnight shift. One Saturday I got a call from Jerry Williams, who ran and owned Trans Maximus (TMI) studios with Steve Cropper. He was the former Business Manager for Paul Revere and the Raiders. Jerry asked me if I wanted to come to the studio. He said one of my favorites was recording there. I had already been there to see Buddy Miles record an album that Cropper produced called *Them Changes*. The title track became

Miles signature song. It also had great versions of Greg Allman's "Dreams" and Neil Young's "Down by the River." I talked to Miles about playing in Jimi Hendrix's Band of Gypsies and some of his experiences playing and recording with the Electric Flag. Michael Bloomfield, another one of my favorites was also in the Electric Flag. I loved him on the *Super Sessions* album he did with Al Kooper and Stephen Stills. Buddy Miles was the first to tell me about Jimi Hendrix giving Stephen Stills guitar lessons.

As it turned out it was indeed one of my favorites, The Jeff Beck Group. Jeff Beck was backed by Max Middleton on Keyboards, Cozy Powell on Drums, Clive Chapman on Bass and Bob Tench on vocals. The same line up that was on the *Rough and Ready* album. Three of them later

Chapter 7: The Last DJ

became members of Hummingbird. I couldn't believe how much Beck and Powell looked alike. It was hard to tell them apart until one of them picked up the guitar. What they were recording turned out to be *The Jeff Beck Group* aka "The Orange Album" that included a song Cropper co-wrote with Beck called "Sugar Cane" and that Don Nix song I mentioned earlier "Going Down."

I also got to meet Reggie Young, another great guitar player when I was working at FM100. I met him when he was working with Chips Moman at American Studio. I watched as Reggie and Chips produced Billy Burnette's first album. Billy was the son of Dorsey Burnette and I didn't realize the connection at the time but Chips got his start in the music business as Dorsey's guitarist. I also met David Hood, Barry Beckett and Roger Hawkins at that session. They gained fame at Muscle Shoals Sound Studios rhythm section. I was only 20 years old and didn't realize that I was in the presence of such great musicians. I had no idea how blessed I was to meet them.

Jon left radio and got into record promotion in a big way. He did local promotion for MCA and then National Album Promotion for ABC Records where he was instrumental in breaking Tom Petty's "Breakdown." MCA bought ABC Records. Jon later became VP of Petty's Backstreet Records.

As I look back at my life I realize that working at FM100 was one of the best jobs I ever had, not to mention one of the most exciting. Radio wasn't always going to be like this, I just didn't know it at the time. All the jocks got every album that came out and good tickets to every concert. That never happens now and all freedom to pick the music you are going to play is also gone. Now, you get a computer printout of what you are going to play. Tom Petty nails the changes in radio with his song "The Last DJ," check out the lyrics. I'm just thankful that I was there for a taste of radio when it was fun and creative. I was one of the last DJ's that got to play what they wanted to play and say what they wanted to say.

Chapter Eight:
Welcome To My Nightmare

Even though I was voted Wittiest in high school I took great pride in never making anyone else the target of my humor. The nerds, the overweight, the less attractive were all safe from my jabs. Living with my mother I knew what it was like to be put down and made fun of. I also took pride in never hitting on or dating my friend's girlfriends or ex-girlfriends. I tried to treat people the way I wanted to be treated.

That's until I laid eyes on a drop dead gorgeous girl that went to Westside, a neighboring high school. She had a perpetual sly grin that drew me to her like a moth to the porch light. She was sarcastic too but as I've always said, "If it ain't sarcastic, it ain't funny." I was very attracted to her. There was just something about her. Only one problem, she was dating a friend of mine named Jerry. He was a little short skinny guy, but he was a badass and heavy into drugs. Once I saw him get into a fight at school. The guy he was fighting was so much taller than he was he had to stand in a chair. He still kicked his ass. I wasn't afraid of him but I did respect him. You know what I mean by respect don't you? Respect is fear with dignity.

Her name was Pat Moore and although she was a little rough around the edges, to me she was a rock star. Even if she wasn't so good lookin', she would still be attractive just because of her demeanor which seemed to say "Impress me." She could make you smile just by looking in your direction. She had long straight brown hair, beautiful brown eyes; cute little dimples when she smiled and just a slight overbite. She was just a living doll.

I had seen Pat a few times at a couple of our hang outs like Krystal's and Filler Burger. She stood out no matter where she was. I couldn't keep my eyes off her. She wore jeans and long sleeve flannel shirts. The reason for the long sleeves would become oblivious later. I discreetly checked her out every chance I got. I never talked to her though, she did a lot of drugs and I was just a pothead. She was cool and didn't seem to think I was that funny. I always noticed, even in a crowd who was laughing and who wasn't. It's like Mark Twain once said "It's better to keep your mouth shut and let people think you are a fool than to open it and remove all doubt." I think as far as she was concerned, I had removed all doubt.

Not long after I started working at FM100, Pat called me. That kind of shocked me. She was crying and told me she was pregnant. "Jerry's in jail and if he finds out he will kill me." Knowing Jerry I knew she was not just taking figuratively. That was a little awkward because although I was attracted to her, I didn't really know her. She was telling me all her personal business. I couldn't figure out why she was doing that. Then "bam" It hit me like a ton of bricks. She, like most people thought DJ's made a lot of money. She wanted to borrow some to go to New York to get an abortion.

Abortions were illegal in Tennessee at the time so she needed five hundred dollars. She promised she would

Chapter 8: Welcome to My Nightmare

pay me back somehow. I was only making sixty dollars a week. So you see, while radio feeds the ego, the family? Not so much. If I saved every penny I made, it would take me two and a half months to have the money to give her. By then she would be thinking of names. I really wanted to help her but I just didn't know how I could.

I weighed all my options and finally came up with a plan. I felt if I could help her now when she desperately needed it, maybe just maybe I would have a chance with her. I know what you're thinking but no, I don't mean get lucky with her. I wanted a relationship. Being her hero when she needed one, that just might do the trick.

The plan I came up with was to ask a friend of mine, an independent record promoter, to loan me the money. I told him she was pregnant with my child. I had to have the money. He thought for a minute. He pushed his glasses up on his forehead as he stroked his beard. The silence seemed to last forever. The suspense was killing me. Everything rested on his decision. I had no one else to turn to for the money. Then, without saying a word he walked over to his safe in his office and handed me five wrapped bundles of five dollar bills marked with his name and $100 on each of them. "This is not a gift" he pointed out "It's a loan and you will have to pay me back." With him being in record promotion and me being a DJ it could look like payola. Neither one of us wanted that.

I didn't hear from Pat for five or six days after I gave

her the money and then she started calling again. We began hanging out together. I felt like she had started to see me for who I was and began to realize how much she meant to me. She knew that I was attracted to her and she was playing me like a drum. I was just too naive to realize it. She told me everything went well with her trip to New York, problem solved. She was no longer pregnant. She didn't want to go into details. I thought that was kind of strange but maybe she was embarrassed about it.

She talked me into letting her drive my car when I was on the air. The one I bought from Betsy's father. One night in a drug induced stupor she hit a telephone pole and put a major dent in the front right fender. She left the scene. I could only hope nobody saw her. She offered me a hundred dollars to pay for it. I thought that was sweet of her until she handed me the money and it was still wrapped with the same bands as the "abortion" money I had given her a couple of weeks earlier. At that point I really felt as if she had just been playing me. I knew she was into some heavy drugs and she would say or do anything to get more. She must have felt something for me by then or at least knew that I really cared about her. If she didn't, she wouldn't have given me back some of the money she conned me out of.

I was still living with my dad then. We had moved into another house and he had remarried. But not to any of those great looking waitresses he went out with. The new house was nothing like the red brick house we lived

Chapter 8: Welcome to My Nightmare

in before the divorce. It was a drab white house made of siding. Like a trailer without the wheels. Did I say trailer? Enter my step mother, Mary. A perfect example of pure redneck trailer trash, she had at least a first grade education and the common sense of a certified accountant. Although she had a son named Sam, dad was her first husband. Until they got married her mother "Big Mama" lived with her and she became a constant house guest in our new home. "Big Mama" tipped the scales at about 350 pounds. She drove a small sedan but she didn't ride in it. She wore it. She chewed, no check that, gummed tobacco. She only had two teeth in her head and they weren't together. She always had a Folgers Coffee can with her to spit in.

"The Frayser House" 1598 Haywood, where I lived growing up

Mary and I didn't get along very well. She made the same mistake that a lot of step parents make. She tried to replace my mom and even she wasn't mean enough to fill that position. How could I treat her as if she was my mother when I didn't even know her? What I did know about her, I didn't like. I don't understand why people think they can demand respect instead of earning it.

One night after working the graveyard shift, Pat and I stopped for some breakfast. We waited until Dad and Mary left for work and Sam was in school before we went to the house. Electric Light Orchestra had just released their first album. I had picked up a copy while we were at the station and put it on the stereo in my bedroom.

While we were listening, we talked. Pat was really starting to open up to me. She told me she had no place to go. She paused looking down into her lap as she sat crosslegged on my bed twirling her long brown hair between her thumb and index finger. As I looked at how beautiful she was, I knew I didn't deserve a girl like her. I knew I was out of my league. She seemed nervous or anxious. Just then she looked up with tears in her eyes, she told me that her step-father had been raping her. My head started to spin as I listened. I couldn't believe what I was hearing. I tried not to show how much that bothered me. I attempted to hide the lump in my throat that I got just hearing about what he had done to her. I wanted to put my arms around her and comfort her but after being raped I thought that may make her feel even more

Chapter 8: Welcome to My Nightmare

uncomfortable. I didn't know what to do. I cared about her. I wanted to do something, but the wrong reaction would destroy the trust she had just put in me.

She told me blow by blow what he had done. He actually thought she was enjoying it. Although he wasn't her natural father he had been a father figure to her for years. Now he was forcing himself on her and expecting her to enjoy it. I wanted to kill him. Pat couldn't tell her mom about it, her mom loved this guy and there was nothing to gain from it. She ran away from home to get away from him. She felt it was her fault, that she may have done something to cause it. There's nothing a woman, or in this case, a girl, can do to deserve being raped. Her life was like a nightmare and she couldn't wake up.

Pat felt all alone and she had to hustle to get money for food and that's why she lied about the abortion. She needed the money to live on. I thought she was playing me and all she was doing was trying to survive. I felt so much closer to her now. She did still have at least a hundred dollars left two weeks later so she had creditability with me. That meant she wasn't squandering it on drugs. She was messed up, but that was her escape from how life had been treating her. I told her that we would come up with a solution somehow. Everything would be okay. How, I didn't know. I just knew I was determined to do something. Coming from my background, I loved to be needed and without a doubt Pat needed somebody.

She said her sister and brother-in-law didn't trust her to live with them because she had stolen a few things from them to pawn to get money to live on. Her actions were screaming out for attention. She had stolen from them so they saw her as a drug addict and a thief. For the first time she was letting me in, being real and trusting me with how she felt. I was beginning to realize she wasn't as hardcore as I thought. Her family was trying to help her. As I found out later they had tried everything else and thought tough love was the best thing for her, it was their last resort.

It was amazing to me that she could trust anyone. Her step-father raped her and she felt nobody in her family trusted her. I never gave up on Pat. I saw something in her eyes. Something rang true as to what she was telling me. She needed someone to believe in her and I was going to be that someone. Maybe she was lying to me. Maybe she was playing me but I had to give her the benefit of doubt. If she was playing me I would find out soon enough. If she wasn't, she trusted me with how she was feeling. I couldn't betray that trust. I was willing to take that chance. I believed she was a good, decent person that had just lost her way. She needed someone to put their faith in her. If I did maybe I could help rebuild her self-esteem the way Mr. Hester had helped me with mine.

The conversation started to taper off. She laid her head on my chest and she fell to sleep as I stoked her hair. I had to show her that I cared and that she could

Chapter 8: Welcome to My Nightmare

trust me. The next thing I knew Sam and Mary were standing at my bedroom door and Mary was screaming at me to wake up. Sam came home from school and saw us. He called Mary and told her I had a girl in bed with me. She left work early to come home and confront us.

Pat and I had left the bedroom door open, we were fully clothed and lying on top of the covers yet Mary was yelling at me "Mitch, Mitch you and your whore get out of that bed." Oh hell no, she did NOT just say that. That really pissed me off because it was all so innocent. After talking to Pat and learning about what she was going through, I wasn't going to allow anybody call her names, especially a whore. It was at that moment I became protective of her.

I jumped off the bed and ran up to the door where they were standing. I got in Mary's face growling at her "How in the hell can you stand there with your fourteen year old bastard and call anyone a whore?" She drew her hand back like she was going to slap me so I pulled my fist back. "If you hit me, I'll tell your daddy" she warned me. Always quick with a comeback, I grinned and said "If I hit you, you won't have to tell him, he'll know you've been hit." Dad had told me in confidence that Mary had not married Sam's father. I had betrayed that trust. I knew it was time for me to move on. I grabbed Pat, left the house and never returned.

We moved in together. I found us an apartment right around the corner from FM100. It was an old two story duplex that had been made into four apartments. It was the early seventies and we couldn't be that open about just living together so we said we were married. I went to the bank to get the deposit money, it had to be in cash. I left Pat there to fill out the application and other paperwork. When I returned to the owner's apartment, I had barely made it through the door when Pat looked at me with a look on her face that said "save me." With that grin I was so fond of on her face she asked "How do you spell McCracken?" I looked at the owner, a blue haired old lady with ruby red lipstick and a unibrow running across her forehead, half of which was raised as if to say this better be good. I just gave her a big smile of confidence and said "Sorry, we're newlyweds." She bought it and we had a place of our own.

Pat and I lived together at 30 South Rembert

Chapter 8: Welcome to My Nightmare

Pat liked to do heroin although she wasn't addicted to it, or at least I told myself that she wasn't. I was trying my best to get her off of it. I started watching who she hung out with. I tried to keep her away from her friends that did hard drugs, just pot which was my drug of choice. I was determined to get her off drugs and turn her life around. The only money coming in was mine which gave me some control over things.

Sometimes I would put on an album side. Anything that was continuous like Crosby, Stills, Nash and Young's *Four Way Street*, Jimi Hendrix's *Electric Ladyland* or any Pink Floyd album and come home for a minute to check on her. Just to make sure she was okay.

I surprised her one night by coming home. She surprised me even more. She was having sex with one of her friends in our bed. I got into a fight with him. She grabbed her clothes, ran into the bathroom and slammed the door. It's easy to win a fight with a naked man. I got him out of the house, but Pat wouldn't open the bathroom door. I let my anger and jealously get the best of me and kicked it in. As the door swung open Pat was giving me a look I had never seen before. It was filled with anger and hate. She was resting her arm over the sink and blood was gushing out of her wrist. She cut it with a razor blade and not just for attention. It was cut to the bone. I had never seen so much blood. I didn't have time to think, just react. I grabbed a towel, wrapped it around her arm and applied pressure to try to stop the bleeding. I knew that she was ashamed of what she had done after I had been taking such good care of her. The drugs were more important to her than I was. She loved drugs, I loved her. She cheated on me, took advantage of me but she was hurt and that was what I cared about at the time. I wasn't sure if I was being good or stupid, maybe a combination of the two, good and stupid.

I called Ron Olson, another DJ who lived right behind the station. He was nice enough to finish my shift for me. Then I rushed Pat to the hospital. On the ride there she told me she didn't care about him. She was just doing it for the drugs. Like that would make it better. So she wasn't cheating, she was just a drug whore? I knew I had to control myself and not turn my back on her the first time she screwed up. I wasn't as mad as I was worried. She lost a lot of blood. After stitching her up, the doctor told me "Just a few more minutes without stopping the bleeding and we could have lost her." If Ron hadn't filled in for me and we had to wait on the ambulance, Pat may have died that night. I told the station I got sick and had to go home.

Pat had a serious problem. I had to move very slowly to help her get away from the heavy drug use. I wasn't a drug counselor, just someone that cared about her. I was trying to get her to stop escaping from life through a drug haze. If I moved too fast she would resist. I had to be nurturing but not controlling. It only took a few months and I was starting to see the results of moving slowly. Pat was starting to do better. She knew I really cared about her. She thought I would be like everyone

Chapter 8: Welcome to My Nightmare

else and turn my back on her. But I didn't, I showed her I truly cared about her. Because of the fact that I believed in her, she started to feel better about herself. I never talked about that night, never threw it up in her face. She started smiling and laughing a lot more. She was getting into music and enjoying my job as a DJ. We started going to more station sponsored concerts and club gigs. We were really starting to enjoy life. I didn't have to share her with so many of her friends. Just a couple that were our friends not just hers, but it wasn't all smooth sailing. She slipped from time to time.

At the time microwave ovens were only in convenient stores and in break rooms at larger companies. We had one at FM100 with a vending machine. I would buy a couple of cherry fried pies, heat them up in the microwave and bring them home, then we put ice cream on them. That was a great treat when you had the munchies.

One morning when I brought the pies home Pat seemed a little more tired than usual, yeah, right tired. None so blind... She had Huckleberry Hound eyes. They were half shut. She stayed up all night when I was working so we would be on the same schedule. I made the munchies for us and before she could take a bite, she told me she had taken sixteen reds (downers). Just then she slumped over and her face went right into the bowl of ice cream. I thought sixteen reds? She deserved whatever happened to her after that. I started to just leave her there but then the newspaper headline flashed into my mind. **FM100 Disc Jockey's Girlfriend Drowns in Bowl of Ice Cream.** That wouldn't be good. So I pulled her out of the ice cream, washed her face, picked her up and put her on the bed. Then I returned to the kitchen and ate them both. Cherry's my favorite.

There was a bar just around the corner on Madison that had opened not long before we moved into our place. They severed one hell of a cheeseburger too. They became known for those cheeseburgers. The place was called Huey's. Pat and I used to go there every Friday night. She loved those burgers as much as I did. We watched as their business grew and grew just by word of mouth. I hated everybody was finding out about "our" place.

We had our tender moments. One of the most memorable was on her birthday. I brought her breakfast in bed. I sat down on the side of the bed and we were talking about going to her sister Shelia's house later in the day and she started to cry. She told me how much she appreciated me helping her get closer to her family, her brother Billy, Sheila and brother-in-law Ronnie but most of all her mother. Her mom had finally seen her husband for the cad he was and kicked him to the curb. She told me she wanted to get a job, get married to a successful man maybe a doctor or a lawyer, have kids and lead a normal life. She wanted to put the drugs behind her and move forward with a more "normal" life. She said she knew that I really loved her and while she appreciated it, she was not in love with me the way I was with her. Like

Chapter 8: Welcome to My Nightmare

any true romantic I thought I would win her over in time.

We had Pat's birthday dinner at Sheila and Ronnie's apartment. It was a great time. Ronnie, Pat and I burned a couple before we ate. Shelia didn't smoke and wasn't thrilled that we were. We drank a few beers, well they did. My dad had put a stop to my drinking a couple of years earlier. It was a good night, a lot of laughs and Pat had some one on one time with Sheila. They had grown much closer over the last few months. It was nice to see Pat laughing and having such a good time with her family. I couldn't help but think about how close I came to losing her just a few months ago to sex, drugs, and ~~rock & roll~~ razor blades. I knew how it felt to lose someone you love and I didn't think I could live through that pain again.

I left at about eleven to go to the station and Pat spent the night with Sheila. Her mother's birthday was just a few days later and we were going to her mom's house the next day to celebrate both birthdays there. I thought about Pat all the way to work, what she had said that morning about not being in love with me. I realized that when she was talking about her future, it didn't include me. She wasn't talking about us getting married and having kids, but marring someone else. After all I was never going to be a lawyer or a doctor, not in this lifetime. That bothered me, but again things had changed so much from when we first met. Who knows what lies in the future for us? I tried to put it out of my mind.

I got to the station and was still feeling the effects of the pot. The good thing about radio back then was that you could play what you wanted to. I was picking out the songs I wanted to play during my shift that night. Not so much the order I would play them in but songs I wanted to play at some point during the night. When you play what you want, you tend to keep the headphones on and listen, get lost in the music. Todd Rundgren was one of my favorites. His *Something Anything* album was still fairly new and I put "Hello, It's Me" on. I still had Pat on my mind and how proud I was of her. I had heard "Hello, It's Me" many times, I had also heard the original version by Rundgren's group the Nazz.

This time, with the day's events on my mind the lyrics took on a whole new meaning, I left the headphones on and just listened to it... it was as if it was for the first time I heard it. *"Hello, it's me I've thought about us for a long, long time. Maybe I think too much but something's wrong. There's something here that doesn't last too long. Maybe I shouldn't think of you as mine."* That was how my day had gone, my thoughts about Pat exactly. I couldn't believe I heard the song so many times and yet never really listened to it. *"Seeing you or seeing anything as much as I do you. I take for granted that you're always there, I take for granted that you just don't care... it's important to me that you know you are free cause I never want to make you change for me."* The song was making me accept the future for us. I cared for her no less, but it gave me acceptance.

Chapter 8: Welcome to My Nightmare

The next day I met Pat at Ronnie and Shelia's and went over to see Pat's Mother. I wasn't making much money. I bought her a mechanical lead pencil. She owned a bar and I thought she may be able to use it. It was overcast that day, misting rain. When she answered the door I was the last one in and I handed the little box to her before I went into the house because I was embarrassed. As I did, I said "I know it's not much, but it's the thought that counts, right?"

Her mom grabbed my wrist so I couldn't walk in. She looked me in the eye. As the mist was hitting both of us in the face, I could tell she was fighting back tears. She said "Mitch, you already gave me something that no one else could give me." As a tear rolled down her cheek, her chin began to quiver as she fought to get the words out "You gave me my daughter back." I gave her a big hug because I knew she got it. She knew I loved her daughter and what I was trying to do. She told Pat later that night that a blind man could see that I was in love with her. That got through to Pat I guess because we made love for the first time that night. I never pushed her for sex because of the rape. It was the first time I ever made love, not the first time I had sex. But the first time I made love.

Pat was getting used to a more normal life and was trying to find a job. It was late August and the Mid South Fair was just around the corner. I suggested that she try to get a job at the fair until she could find a full time job somewhere else. Within days she had one. She worked in a booth where they made the chocolate dipped ice cream bars and rolled them in crushed peanuts. She was working long hours and since we lived a few doors down from the station, she used my car to go back and forth to the fairgrounds. I just walked to work.

One night I had to emcee a concert at the Overton Park Shell, an open air arena in the Midtown area of Memphis. I think it was Procol Harum. I had to use the car. I drove her to work and she was going to try to get a ride home from the fairgrounds with one of her coworkers.

I was worried because there was a black serial rapist that had raped two white women in Memphis. That was unusual because at the time, of all rapes only five percent were interracial. The rapist would beat the women, steal their purses, strip them and put them out in a bad part of town. One of the women was raped again before she could find help. He would force the women into his car with a butcher knife. Once they were in, there was no door handle or window crank. They were trapped.

Pat couldn't get a ride so she hitchhiked. She was looking good in her tight jeans and a halter top so only one or two cars passed before one pulled up to offer her a ride. It was a black man who was kind enough to get out and open the door for her so she could get in. As he shut the door for her Pat realized why. There was no door handle on the inside. The window crank was missing too. As he opened his door and the dome light came on she saw a butcher knife stuck into his armrest.

Chapter Nine:
Alone

As Pat was getting into his car I was calling the house to see if she had made it home ok. There was no answer and I was getting worried. I told myself that maybe she had to work a little over to calm myself down enough to concentrate on my air shift.

I may have been worried but Pat was more terrified than any time in her life. She realized that the serial rapist preying on the women of Memphis for the last two weeks by all likelihood had just trapped her inside his rape chamber, and she was all alone.

As soon as he entered the car she demanded to be let out. When he refused, Pat dove across him to grab the knife getting an elbow in the face for her trouble. That knocked her back against the seat. She used the momentum of bouncing off the seat to go for his throat with her nails. She was scratching and ripping at his neck and face. He started hitting her in the face with his fist as she scrabbled to get her feet up on the seat. When she did she dove backwards into the backseat hoping she could escape the car from one of the backdoors. As her shoulders hit the seat, he was right on top of her continuing the beating. She tried to block his punches with her arms and covered her face. He grabbed a hand full of her hair and pulled her head back to continue his assault on her. He ripped out handfuls of her hair as he did. He got one more clear shot at her face and punched her right in the month. The pain was excruciating as she felt not only the pain of the knuckles making contact but she also felt one of her front teeth snapping and being ripped from her mouth.

She felt her head start to throb as the beating continued, she was barely conscious. He positioned her across the backseat as she moaned in pain. She felt him unbuckle her belt. She put her hands on his to try to prevent the inevitable but her strength was gone. He just pushed her hands away as he pulled her belt out of her jeans and tied her hands behind her back with it. With her hands behind her back it elevated her and made access easier for him. He pressed his cheek against hers as he snarled "You have no defense now. If you fight me or try to prevent me from doing this I will really hurt you. This is going to happen." As she heard him unzip her jeans she turned her head toward the back of the seat and started to cry. What had she done to deserve such a severe beating and being raped again? He pulled her pants and panties off and spread her legs open.

I was at the station trying to do my shift when an eerie feeling came over me. A chill ran up my spine and the hair on my arms was standing up. I just felt something was so terribly wrong. I called the house again, and once again there was no answer.

At the time I was calling my worst fear was taking place. Pat was being raped. After he raped her he stripped off the rest of her clothes, piling them up on the floorboard and raped her once more.

Chapter 9: Alone

When he was finished with her he forced her back into the front seat and tossed her purse to the back with her clothes. He gave her nothing to cover up with, so she curled up in the fetus position covering herself as best she could. He started to drive away. He drove her to one of the worst parts of town. He pulled up and parked on a side street. Pat just assumed it was his house and he was going to take her in, rape her at least one more time and possibly kill her. She kept telling herself that none of the other women he raped had been killed. That gave her a ray of hope that she would live to see that he paid for what he did to her. He got out of the car. Pat was relieved to see that the knife was still stuck down into the armrest. She thought about trying to grab it before he got to her door but she was hurting all over and just didn't have the strength to try. He opened her door, reached in, grabbed her by the hair of the head and literally tossed her to the curb. She rolled up into a ball and watched to see if he was going for the knife. He got in his car and drove off leaving her raped, beaten and nude in the worst place she could be.

It was about two in the morning by then. Pat looked around and the street was quiet, no movement at all. She saw a house across the street with a light on in what looked like a bathroom. She studied it for a few minutes and then the light went out. Someone was up in that house. Maybe she could get help. What if it's a man and a naked girl comes knocking on his door? Will she be raped again like the story in the newspaper? Even if it's a woman she could slam the door in her face for fear of getting involved.

She knew she would have to do it now if she was going to do it at all. She decided it was worth a chance and pounded on the door screaming as loud as she could "Help me please, somebody help me!" That way if she was in trouble at that house maybe someone else will hear and help. She saw the light in the living room turn on. As the door opened in what seemed to be slow motion, she saw a short portly black woman looking through the storm door at her. Her hair was rolled in pink sponge hair rollers wrapped in a red scarf. As she looked to see who was causing all the commotion on her front porch. Pat could see the worry and kindness in her eyes and she knew her ordeal was over.

The woman opened the storm door to usher Pat into the safety of her home. Her name was Shirley Brown. She sent her husband Charles out to make sure he was gone. Shirley wrapped a blanket around Pat, but had the good sense to not let her wash off. She knew the police would need pictures and to do a rape kit before she could do that.

I was worried sick about Pat by then. I had been calling the house for hours and not getting an answer. Pat should have been home by one at the latest. In addition to being worried about her safety I felt so responsible if anything did happen to her because I was the one who suggested she work at the fair and I had to use the car that night. I was sitting listening to Loggins

Chapter 9: Alone

and Messina's "Trilogy" when I saw the phone light blinking. I dove for the phone hoping to hear Pat's voice. "Hi, FM100...who's this" I said praying it would be Pat saying she was home and safe. "It's me baby" Pat said with a shaky and muffled voice. I could hear the terror, "What's wrong Pat, are you okay?" "No, I've been raped and had the crap beaten out of me. The police are on the way. I'm at a nice lady's house, she and her husband saved me."

"Oh my God Pat, I'm so sorry. Do you want me to come to be with you? I can get someone to finish the shift for me."

"No, I'm okay now and the police just got here. I'll call you back before you get off the air." She hung up the phone as my eyes welled up. I exhaled and it felt like my life had just left my body.

I felt terrible, this is the worst possible news I could get. It was all I could do to continue my shift. Pat called me just before I got off the air. She was at the hospital and had done an interview with a couple of detectives. She was ready to come home and take a warm bath. I rushed to get her as soon as my replacement got there.

I picked her up at the hospital. She didn't look as bad as I thought she would. She said she looked much worse when she first got to the hospital. On the way home I couldn't apologize enough. Pat told me that I had done nothing wrong and couldn't have known what was going to happen. While it was good to hear, it did little to ease my guilt.

When we got to the house Pat couldn't get into the tub fast enough. I wanted to give her the privacy I felt she needed after going through such an ordeal. I wanted to just hold her and tell her how much I loved her. But I knew this was not the time. As she bathed I just paced the floor as the tears flowed from my eyes. I had held it back as long as I could. Pat had done so well in her recovery. This could send her in downward spiral. I was really worried about her.

She had been in the bathroom for a long time. I could hear her talking. I got myself together, as I approached the door I could make out what she was saying "I'm dirty, I'm dirty, I'm dirty." I could hear the water splashing. I opened the door and saw she was scrubbing herself with a wire brush. The water was pink with blood. I grabbed a bath towel, threw it around her shoulders and pulled her out of the bathtub. She was facing me and started screaming and hitting me repeatedly in the face with her fists. I just wrapped my arms around the small of her back and allowed her to continue to hit me until she got all the anger out. When she did she just laid her exhausted head on my shoulder and began to cry. I continued to hold her. She began to tell me as best she could what he had done to her.

I moved her to the bed and we both sat down on the side of it. I told her none of what happened was her fault

Chapter 9: Alone

that she wasn't dirty. She felt so violated, so used and then tossed away like a bag of garbage.

She asked me if I still wanted to make love to her. "Of course, Pat" I said "I love you and what happened to you does not change that, nothing will." "Even now" she asked meaning after being raped. I pulled the towel back to expose her bloody crotch and said "I don't think now would be so good for you." That cracked her up, "I can't believe you can make me laugh even now" she said as she reached out and put her arms around my neck. She gave me a tender kiss. I stood up and then bent down and kissed her wound. Not in a sexual way, just a quick peck to let her know that to me she was not dirty or soiled. Then I went to get some first aid supplies to clean her up. As I headed to the bathroom she said "Thanks for letting me beat the crap out of you, believe it or not that really helped."

The serial rapist got three other women after Pat before being captured. I talked to the cops that arrested him and they said he pulled up next to them at a red light. They had such a good description of him and his car that they knew right away he was their guy. The cop riding shotgun looked over in his direction and he just stared straight ahead. The officer told me "Nobody does that unless they don't want to make eye contact with a cop. The only reason to do that's because you are guilty of something," he went on to say "I checked out his face and then his car, that's when I realized who he was. I looked at my partner and said Look who we got here as I pulled out my pistol. I opened my door, his window was rolled down so I put my gun to his temple and told him if he moved a muscle I would kill him on the spot. A crowd began to gather as I opened his door to pull him out. When I did I saw the knife right where Pat and the other women said it would be, stuck in the arm rest."

Pat had her good days and bad, she was on an emotional roller coaster. She finally gave up and started doing heroin again to escape the horror of what happened to her and the trauma of the upcoming trial. The drugs were once again more important than I was. They eventually won the battle for her so we went our separate ways.

Whenever I was really missing her, I would go back to Huey's and order that cheeseburger. I would just think about all the good times we had. It was as if she was right there with me. Huey's was still "our" place.

Pat was not out of my life for good though, at least not yet. Everything happens for a reason, God never gives you more than you can handle and Pat could handle a lot more than even I thought she could.

Chapter Ten:
Against All Odds

After a few years of doing the graveyard shift at FM100 and with Pat out of my life, I was ready for a change. Sure I was making a name for myself in my hometown but I wanted more. I wanted to spread my wings a bit so I found a job as a Program Director in Beaumont, Texas at KWIC. I was hired to take the station from a Top 40 format to Album Rock. Right up my alley.

The station under the Top 40 format had sold a contract to a seventy some odd year old conservative, naïve, opinionated church lady to do a talk show between noon and one Monday through Friday. The first day I was there I checked her out.

There was nothing I could do, she was already under contract. She was paying for the airtime but I was dying to hear what she sounded like. Well guess what? She sounded just like you may think, like my grandmother on the air.

The state of Texas had just changed the marijuana laws from an average of twenty years per joint to a mere fine for a full ounce of pot. She was talking about that and she just didn't get how much an ounce was. A guy called in who was an experienced pot smoker and she asked "How many marijuana 'cigarettes' do you get from an ounce. "He laughed and said "That depends on how big you roll 'em you stupid bitch." Needless to say there was no delay.

I was doing afternoons and one day I accidently kicked the power cord to the turntables and didn't realize it. All I knew is that I couldn't get them to work. I started taking phone calls and would talk about whatever the caller wanted to talk about. I knew at some point someone would call in and want to talk about drugs or try to get their favorite four letter word over the air. Sure enough when I answered the fourth or fifth call the caller said "Dude, you know where I can get a bag?" Without missing a beat I answered "Right here Monday through Friday from noon to one" and went to the next call. Of course the call after that was from her daughter and she was not pleased.

KWIC was the first Album Rock station in Beaumont. Before the change of format KLOL in Houston was the only Album Rock station around. I was doing some Major Market promotions in a Small Market. I knew how to work the record companies for concert tickets (in Houston), trips, etc. I reported to as many trade magazines as I possibly could. That made the station much more important to the record companies. It gave me more of a priority with them. One of the trades was the Bob Hamilton and Friends Radio Report, more on that later.

The Station was making a name for itself not only in Beaumont but throughout the whole region. In fact I got a call one day to emcee a concert in Lake Charles, La. I knew the opening act was going to be War who had just released *The World is a Ghetto* album, their hit from it was

Chapter 10: Against All Odds

"The Cisco Kid."

It was a Friday night and I was back stage talking to the promoter of the show when all of a sudden the headliners dressing room door opened and out walks B.B. King. I couldn't believe it. Love the man...you know, Memphis Music and all. I used to hear him on the radio when I was growing up.

The promoter introduced me as a Program Director from Beaumont and B.B. stuck his hand out and said "What cha say, Mitch?" "WDIA" I replied. That's the station that B.B. worked for years ago. With an almost blank look on his face he said "You from Memphis?" "Yes sir, I used to hear you promoting your shows at The Peanut Club." We talked for about 45 minutes and he told me the story of how he named his guitar Lucille.

It seems he was playing a club in Twist, Arkansas, a "Colored" club he called it. It was cold and the only heat in the club was a big barrel of burning oil. Two men were trying to get the attention of the same woman and got into a fight over her. In the struggle they knocked the barrel over and set the club on fire. B.B. got out safe and realized he left his guitar in the burning building so he ran back in to get it. He barely got out before the building collapsed. I'm sure you have figured out by now the girl they were fighting over was named Lucille.

Beaumont and neighboring Port Arthur, Texas were very rich in music history. Johnny and Edgar Winter are

From Beaumont and so is The Big Bopper (aka JP Richardson). He was the disc jockey turned singer who wrote and recorded "Chantilly Lace." Janis Joplin is from Port Arthur, just seventeen miles away. I got into the Texas Blues scene there and went to a lot of clubs to see some of the blues artist. Many times I was the only white man there but everyone went for the same reason, the music. As long as I left their women alone we were good.

KWIC's AM station was an R&B station, so we were the two elements that the citizens of Beaumont hated the most, blacks and hippies. Not necessarily in that order because hippies chose to be who they were. One day, one of the AM jocks was shot at from across the street. The bullet barely missed him. I drove back to Memphis the next day.

One of the trade magazines I reported to at KWIC as I mentioned was The Bob Hamilton and Friends Radio Report. Bob had just moved his magazine from LA to Memphis. I called before leaving Beaumont and had a job as a researcher waiting on me when I got home. The job sounds impressive but I just called radio stations across the country to get their charts and compile our national charts for Album Radio, Top 40, Adult Contemporary, R&B and Country. The magazine went to about 1300 Radio Stations all over the country.

Bob Hamilton ran the magazine from his home. At a party there, I met a record promoter named Bill Browder. Bill had black hair and a thick beard, he was an

Chapter 10: Against All Odds

independent record promoter who had worked with RCA Records and helped break songs like Elvis Presley's "Suspicious Minds" and John Denver's "Take Me Home Country Roads" among others. He was telling me about how at one time he had a recording contract with Atlantic Records under the name Brian Stacy and had opened shows for the Beach Boys. He also said he had come across a demo for a song called "Devil in the Bottle" and was trying to find someone to record it.

3022 Old Brownsville Road "home" of the Bob Hamilton and Friends Radio Report.

The next time I talked to Bill he had shaved his beard off, changed his name to TG Sheppard and recorded the song himself. I have heard that TG stands for "The Good" Sheppard. But the story I heard was Bill was standing in his living room, looking out his bay window trying to think of a name when a German Sheppard walked across his yard. That was how TG Sheppard was born, from The German Sheppard.

I mentioned that album stations back then were called progressive or cosmic. While I was working for The Hamilton Report I met a young radio programmer that would change the format forever and for the better, his name was Lee Abrams.

Lee was only 22 and had come up with an Album Rock format called "Superstars." He had a couple of stations signed up already. One of them was in Louisville, KY. My old friend from WHBQ, Robert W. Walker was The Program Director there at WLRS. Rob was not only one of the best jocks I ever heard, he also knew the business of radio. He stayed on the cutting edge of changes in the industry and was always on top of things. So if Lee was ok with Rob he had to know what he was doing.

Lee looked even younger than his years, thin with curly black hair. He was impressive. He was one of the most intelligent radio guys I had ever talked to. In fact he was so smart, he was hip. He was focused on what he was doing and had an unbelievable drive to get it done.

Chapter 10: Against All Odds

We talked about what he was doing and about the two stations I had worked with. For me it had always been about the music. Lee was talking about really cool features for the stations. Like album hours, featured artist of the day, mini concerts, etc. I had never thought about that much. His excitement for what he was doing was contagious. For Lee it wasn't just the music, it was the image that would make the stations and the format succeed. He went on to add over two hundred stations as clients. He went on to become Senior VP and Chief Creative Officer for XM Satellite Radio.

Lee made me really miss being on the air so after about three months I was itching to get back into radio. About that time I heard from one of my best friends from high school, George Bryant who also went into radio. He was programming a station in Florence, Ala and wanted me to come to work for him. I was tired of doing the phone work and was ready to get back on the air. So I took him up on his offer.

What I didn't know at the time was that the station was owned by Sam Phillips of Sun Records. The Florence-Lauderdale Coliseum was right across the street from the station, WQLT. I emceed a concert there with the Charlie Daniels Band opening for the Marshal Tucker Band. Charlie came to the station for an interview with two of his band members each carrying a bucket of Kentucky Fried Chicken under each arm. It was while I was at WQLT that I met a model's little sister who told me a story about How Ronnie Van Zant of Lynyrd

Skynyrd wrote "Mississippi Kid" for her sister. Really? That story was a little hard to swallow but I did remember it.

I just got off the air one Saturday afternoon and walked into the lobby when I saw Mr. Phillips standing there. I found out in short order that he prefers Sam rather than Mr. Phillips. He sat down with me and we talked about a lot of things. He told me that Radio was his first love, not recording. In fact the recording started as a sound effects library for radio production and it grew from there. Sun Studios was originally called The Memphis Recording Studio with the slogan "We Record Anything, Anywhere, Anytime."

I just had to ask Sam about selling Elvis' contract for $40,000. Sam said "Well first of all it was $45,000, Elvis got $5,000. Secondly that was a lot of money back in 1955 especially for an artist that had never had a hit. Money I could use to promote Roy Orbison, Jerry Lee Lewis, Johnny Cash and Carl Perkins." I knew Elvis had started on Sun but didn't realize he had never had a hit with them. I asked about how Carl Perkins felt about Elvis recording "Blue Suede Shoes" a song Perkins wrote and had recorded himself. Sam said "Well back then the best way to sell records was by touring. Carl had been in a car wreck and couldn't tour. Elvis also had a hit with it bringing in money Carl would have never seen from royalties." After two hours or so Sam said "You know, I usually get paid for these interviews." "Well considering what you pay me, let's just call it even" I said with a

Chapter 10: Against All Odds

smirk. We both laughed and walked out to the parking lot together. As we did Sam asked "What do I pay you anyway?" "Not enough" was my only reply. Sam was a living legend and yet he was so down to earth, a really great man. It was pleasure to meet and to work for him.

I wrote an article about that conversation for an online publication, the Examiner back in August of 2009. Seems every Elvis website in the world posted it.

Out of the blue one day I got a call from Bob Hamilton who wanted to sell the Magazine so he could return to LA. He said he wanted to sell it to me because I was young and he believed in me. He also said he knew I believed in what the magazine was doing. I returned to Memphis to buy the magazine and changed the name to Radio Magazine. I brought George in as a full partner. We predicted hits on the back cover and put the hits on the inside cover. I put this one particular song on the back cover and got all kinds of calls from Program Directors all over the country. They were telling me what an idiot I was because the groups last two singles stiffed (didn't sell). I was twenty-four years old and all these old farts were calling me and telling me I didn't know what the hell I was talking about. Long story short, the record was "Rikki Don't Lose That Number," to this day the biggest hit Steely Dan has ever had. Let me say it one more time, I told you so!

I did a lot of interviews at the magazine the most notable being a Program Director at WPEZ in Pittsburg.

He went on to program WNBC in New York and then on to Warner Brothers Cable to start up a little network called MTV, his name was Bob Pittman. He later became the President and COO of another company that changed how we all communicate with each other called AOL!

The staff of Radio Magazine back in 1974. From left Melody Haspel, Mitch McCracken, Leslie Alexander, Joe Milner, Karen Moore, Rusty Hill, Christy Conlee and Bruce Bowles.

I also interviewed a Program Director of the #1 station in Charlotte, North Carolina, WAYS. The Station had been #1 for ten years. He told me they had just done some research and found that no one listened to the station. His point was that you decide what you want to know and then justify it with research. So by asking the right people you can find that the #1 station has no

Chapter 10: Against All Odds

listeners. His name is Jay Thomas. You may remember him as Eddie LeBec, the hockey-player-turned-traveling-ice show-skater second husband of Carla on Cheers in the late 80's. He also appeared on Murphy Brown as a talk show host, Jerry Gold, who was one of Murphy's many lovers. She went through as many lovers as she did secretaries if you remember.

At that time there was a two or three block strip on Madison Ave in Memphis called Overton Square. It was the happening place in Memphis. There were clothes shops, restaurants, etc. If it was hip, it was at Overton Square. There was also a live music club called Lafayette's Music Room. I was invited there two weeks in a row to see two completely different acts. The first week the invitation came from a little label called Bell Records (soon to become Arista) I saw Barry Manilow who did a medley of his "Greatest Hits" all commercial Jingles. He wrote the "You Deserve a Break Today" jingle for McDonalds, State Farm Insurance, Dr. Pepper, and Kentucky Fried Chicken among others. At the time his claim to fame was as Bette Midler's music director.

The next week the invitation came from Casablanca Records and their act didn't have an album deal yet, just a single. George Klein was also there to see them. Their Promotion Man handcuffed George to a pole in the club so he couldn't walk out on them. I thought they were going to be terrible if he had to trap people there. As it turned out it, that was not necessary at all. The Group was Kiss. After the show I interviewed Gene Simmons and Paul Stanley for the magazine. Things were going pretty well with the magazine. I was only 24 and I had two houses and three cars. Life was not only good, it was fun.

A friend who was doing promotion for one of the major labels invited me to go to Little Rock to a concert. Target, a Memphis group was opening for one of his acts. He came by the house to pick me up. We were driving to the show.

When he arrived he had a date with him and she wasn't his wife. She was however a beautiful girl. She had an olive complexion and blue eyes. She wore just enough eye makeup to make them stand out. She had a models figure, slim but not skinny that was soft and sensuous to the touch. She was one of those people that had to touch you when she talked to you. I drug out each conversation as long as I could. Her name was Rose Heller and she was from Germany. I asked her if she was related to Kelen Heller but she didn't get it, she didn't know who Helen Keller was and had never seen the Miracle Worker.

We went backstage and partied before the show. That's where I first met Jimi Jamison who was then the lead singer of Target. He later replaced Dave Bickler in Survivor. When I was backstage before the show I was introduced to one of the groupies, her name was Connie. "Not Sweet, Sweet Connie from American Band," she just smiled and licked her lips. "Sweet, Sweet Connie

Chapter 10: Against All Odds

doin' it right" I said with a grin, it was a JOKE! At least I thought it was. "Are you in the band" she asked. "No" is all I could get out before she snapped "No head for you." In hindsight she sounded a lot like the Soup Nazi.

We partied backstage again after the show and stayed too late and drank and smoked too much to drive home so we decided to get a couple of hotel rooms. Rose and her date had a room that connected to mine. I settled down for the night and was about to turn off the light when there was a soft knock at the door. It wasn't the front door, it was the adjoining door. I was in my boxers so I just opened it a crack and there stood Rose. "Can I share your room with you" she asked. My friend was a nice looking guy who had some great connections in the music business so I was a bit shocked. "Why" I asked. "Because I feel safer with you than I do with him," she explained "This is the first time I've gone out with him and I wasn't planning on spending the night. He may try something and I don't think you will." "Now how in the hell am I supposed to take that" I asked with a smile, "As a compliment or a slam?" "Whatever it takes to get me in there" she said with a wink. I let her in even though I was only wearing my boxers. When I answered the door I was fine but now I had a place to hang my hat.

That was a great night we shared the same bed and while we didn't have sex we did a lot of cuddling and slept in each other's arms. She looked like a Victoria's Secret model and was wearing about as much to sleep in. She rested her head on my chest as I laid on my back. She threw her leg across me, oh my God it was so soft and warm to the touch. Her leg came almost up to my waist so I know she could feel my attraction for her. I wasn't sure if she was trying to seduce me or not but I liked the fact that she felt safe with me. I didn't do anything to change that. I knew we were both single and lived in Memphis so if she was interested we would have other opportunities. If she wasn't interested she would just turn me down anyway. I hate getting turned down.

It was just a few days later. Rose had given me her card. She told me she enjoyed meeting me and to feel free to give her a call whenever I wanted. I didn't want to seem too eager but I was thinking of calling her to see if she would go out with me when the phone rang. I smiled because I just knew it was Rose, I have a sense about these things. I answered the phone anticipating that sweet sounding German accent but I got a big surprise instead. "Mr. Mitch McCracken" the voice on the other end asked. "Yes" I answered, "Please hold for Attorney General Hugh Stanton." Why in the world would the Attorney General want to talk to me? This couldn't be good, right? He asked me to come in and meet with him.

I went in to see Mr. Stanton. His desk was as wide as most are long and he tossed me a picture. "Do you know her" he asked. I looked at it and it was Pat, the girlfriend that had been raped almost three years ago by a serial rapist. She had a missing tooth, two black eyes, and some of her hair had been pulled out. "Yes sir" I admitted "I know her, but I swear I didn't do this." It turns out that it

Chapter 10: Against All Odds

was the picture the police took after her rape. Three years had passed and I never saw her until after she was cleaned up.

"We know who did it and quite frankly Mitch we need your help convicting him. Pat's at the Memphis House (a rehab center) and she's still getting drugs. I need her straight so I can use her testimony. Her mother said you are the only one that can get her off drugs. I want to release her into your custody, what do you say?"

"Like I would say no to the Attorney General, I'm not sure I can work the same magic but I'll try."

I was interested in Rose but as it turned out she was engaged. She told me she was ending it. I gave her space to take care of business and Pat came to live with me at a time when I could afford to show her a good time. I knew if I could show her love and support, that's all it took to get her off the drugs. They were her escape. When she first moved in I took her shopping. I spent a lot of money buying her clothes, jewelry, shoes, whatever she wanted. It made both of us feel great, me better than her I think. I was still in love with her and I wanted her to know it.

I went through the trial with her every step of the way. When she was on the stand she looked that son-of-a-bitch right in the face and told the court what he did to her. He of course pleaded innocent. His attorney was trying to make Pat look bad. He asked her if she ever hitchhiked. She gave him a cold stare and asked "No, why?" He had nowhere to go with that line of questioning. I was so proud of her. His client was thirty-four years old and was sentenced to sixty-seven years with no possible parole, off the streets for good.

After the trial Pat told me she couldn't express how much she appreciated all I've done for her. Here it comes, the "I appreciate you speech." When it starts out like that, you end up on the curb and I did. Pat said she just wasn't in love with me. It hurt but I had no choice, I had to let her go. I had that stupid poster in my bedroom "If you love something set it free...if it's meant to be....yadda yadda yadda." That doesn't help when you're hurting. But you know what did help? Rose. She had split up from her fiancé and we started seeing each other. We went out to eat, to movies, concerts and then just started spending a lot of time at the house.

I would check on Pat from time to time to see how she was doing and make sure she wasn't back sliding. One of our mutual friends told me she was back at the Memphis House. I hung up and immediately called her dad, not her stepfather but her real dad. "How's Pat doing" I asked. "Mitch, you wouldn't believe it, she's like a different person" he said and he sounded so cheerful. "Well, I talked to one of her friends and she said Pat was back at the Memphis House." "Really," he said sounding a little irritated, "Did she tell you she was a staff member now, a counselor? She just gave notice and is going to the Methodist Hospital to work with their Methodist Outreach Program. She's going to be in charge of all

Chapter 10: Against All Odds

juvenile counseling. They bypassed three people with degrees to get her. You can't lie to her. She's been there."

A few years later I heard she had her own practice. She was married, to a lawyer I believe, and had two little boys. All the things she told me on her birthday had come true. I couldn't be happier or more proud of her. I've never tried to contact her because I think I would be a reminder of a time that she would just as soon forget. When I first met Pat I wanted to be her hero. As it turned out, she was one of mine. She's every woman who has ever pulled herself up by her bootstraps and succeeded against all odds. She was raped, beaten, strung out on drugs and yet she pulled herself out of the ashes with her head held high. She has helped many people over the years live better and more productive lives. Including her own brother, Billy, who has been sober now for twenty-eight years.

When I think back about Pat, I still see that cute nineteen year old girl that was so beautiful and so very cool. Who had that sly smile with just a bit of a snarl. The girl who sat on my bed, opened up and trusted me even though she barely knew me. But I also see the strong, intelligent and independent woman that she became. The young girl who wanted to be trusted became a woman that showed other drug addicts how to become trustworthy and how they too could do the right thing.

I was disappointed when she didn't need me to watch over her anymore. But I was also proud of her for the same reason. She became more dependent on herself. She became the master of her own destiny. She learned how to help herself and taught others to do the same.

Pat would never have reached her goals with me and she had the sense to know it, even if I didn't. She is one of the strongest, most determined women I have ever known. How could you not love and admire a woman like Pat Moore?

Chapter Eleven:
Going Down

Being the owner and editor of Radio Magazine was a lot of fun. I loved doing the interviews, going to the concerts and the interaction with Program Directors from all over the country. As staff member Melody Haspel recently pointed out "We were all like rock stars ourselves back then. It was an awesome time for all of us." But the short ride was about to come to an abrupt end.

Stax Records and Union Planters Bank embezzled Radio Magazine from me. Stax was into the bank to the tune of 10.5 million dollars in 1974. That's a lot of money now but even more back then. I just got a feeling that things weren't right with the bank. I was dealing with the Executive Vice President, Joe Harwell. Why was the Executive VP my loan officer in the first place? That in itself should have been a red flag. He told me he wasn't going to credit my account anymore as the checks came in. He was going to wait until they cleared the bank they were written on. That just didn't sound right to me. We were operating on a shoestring and that ended my cash flow for at least ten days.

I heard from some music business insiders in Memphis that Stax was somehow involved in the magazine. I called Attorney General Hugh Stanton and asked him to look into it for me. I had helped him by getting Pat straight enough to testify in the rape case, so I thought he might help me out. He said he would look into it but made no promises.

When Phil Canale stepped down as Attorney General, he accepted the position as President of Union Planters Bank. Mr. Stanton didn't need a search warrant. He just called his former boss and had him look over the loan papers from the inside.

Mr. Stanton called me the next day and asked me who the cosigner on my $60,000 loan was. When I said "No one cosigned the loan" there was a brief pause. Then he said "Okay, I'm turning this over to the FBI."

He went on to tell me that Al Bell and Stax Records were cosigners on the note. The loan was set up in such a way that if they had to make any payment at all, the magazine would become their property. That's why Joe Harwell froze my account. By not crediting my account when the checks came in, there were no funds available. My note was due three days later so Stax would have to make the payment and then could take control of the magazine.

According to court documents, *in November 1973 Joe Harwell discussed with his superior at the bank, the idea of taking a leave of absence for six months to work on a "Memphis Music" show for national television. He was also to develop a personal business called "Action for Ideas." The business was to function as a financial advisor to the music industry. After its establishment Harwell was to resume his duties with the bank.*

It was about that time that I got my loan to buy the

Chapter 11: Going Down

magazine, along with my partner and high school friend George Bryant. The "Memphis Music" TV show of course never happened. But Harwell did rape the Memphis Music industry. In my opinion Joe Harwell was not only directly responsible for the downfall of Stax Records, but also for the decline of Memphis Music in general.

Those same court documents made it clear what kind of man Joe Harwell was. *He authorized loans for Stax Records from Union Planters Bank in return he received cash payments to himself from Stax. In addition, in the early sixties Harwell began to set up fictitious accounts, without the involvement of Stax, and made loans to them and directly embezzled the money.*

When my account at Union Planters screeched to a halt, I had just written a check to the Post Office for our Pitney Bowes postage machine. I bounced a check for $1,300 to the government. Big Brother doesn't take kindly to being screwed out of over a thousand dollars.

Mr. Stanton told me there would be a federal warrant issued for my arrest. The charge would be Check Fraud. His investigation into Joe Harwell and Al Bell was continuing and he didn't want me to be arrested. My innocence would prove wrong doing by the bank. That would expose his investigation. He suggested that I curtail any phone calls and/or letters to anyone. I needed to become invisible so the investigation could continue. until the investigation was completed. I thought an out of town job would be a good idea about now.

In the meantime Lee Abrams had set me up with the owner of the station he was consulting in New Orleans, WRNO. So off to the Crescent City I went.

WRNO flew me down to meet with them about the job. I was excited to be going back on the air and to be in New Orleans was a dream come true. To be anywhere but Memphis at the time was not only a thrill but a necessity.

I always fly in the window seat if I can. It's a short flight to New Orleans, as we approached the New Orleans airport the plane banked over the city and I looked down to take it all in. As I did I died laughing. Someone had climbed on top of the Superdome and painted "714"in big black numbers right in the middle of the top of the dome. It looked like a giant Quaalude right in the middle of the city. How cool was that? I knew then this going to be my next great adventure and I was right. It was going to be one hell of a ride, but a little bumpier than I thought.

Meeting Joe Costello, the owner was a trip. Joe was a giant in New Orleans Radio. He was also a giant in the hallway. He weighed at least 400 lbs. You could actually feel him walking down the hall to the conference room. He wasn't a tall man, about 5' 5" standing up or lying down. He had dark brown hair with a few strands combed over the top of his bald head. He looked like an

Chapter 11: Going Down

Italian Dick Van Patton. Joe smiled a lot and was very charismatic. He was a great guy and seemed like he was going to be easy to work for.

Once it was determined that I had the job he taught me how to pronounce New Orleans. There are no counties in the state, it's catholic. New Orleans was in Orleans Parrish. So if you were talking about the Parrish it was pronounced with two syllables Orleans. But New Orleans was pronounced N'awlins as one word. He then took me to lunch. We went to a Cajun restaurant in the French Quarter. He treated me to my first bowl of red beans and rice, seafood gumbo and bread pudding. I knew I was going to love it there. Food was my life. I could eat and eat and never gain a pound. I was twenty three then, by the time I turned thirty two, everything I ate before showed up.

I returned to Memphis to pack up the car and drive back because I had to get the hell out of Dodge before the Postal Inspector could find me. Joe set me up with the Causeway Hotel, where the radio station was, so I would have a place to stay until I found my own place.

With the impending downfall of the magazine I was going to lose my houses and cars. I was going down big time. From being worth about a half million dollars to natta. I was going to have to start all over again but I was okay with that. Life was nothing but an adventure then. No promises, no regrets.

Radio Daze

Things were going well with Rose and she wanted to move with me so we were going to use her car. But before I left, I had a lot of business to take care of.

What was my staff going to think if I just didn't show up at work? The office would be filled with Feds and Police looking for me. The Bank and Stax would be there to seize the magazine.

When George and I first took over the magazine, his wife was working at Shoney's Restaurant corporate office. We needed a computer to compile the music that we got from our reporting stations. There weren't many computers at the time but Shoney's was nice enough to let us use theirs on Friday afternoon. The mailing list and billing list were on the cards we used to input the information.

I asked Mr. Stanton if I could get in touch with the staff to let them know what was going on. He thought that the less they knew the better off they would be.

Stax and Union Planters would have my office, my equipment, my staff...everything they needed to publish the magazine. Stax owed Union Planters millions of dollars. They both had motivation to get the magazine from me. They could then make Stax records look good. Thereby getting more airplay which would lead to more sales and getting out of debt. That was the plan anyway.

What could the little man do against the big machine?

Chapter 11: Going Down

Well, first of all the little man was from Frayser. A somewhat bad part of town where there were lots of fights and plenty of violence. Anytime you grow up in that kind of environment and you're not tough, you have to think fast on your feet. I was never tough but I had a quick wit and a lot of common sense that I picked up from Dad.

So here's what the little man decided to do on his way out the door. I went to the office on Sunday afternoon and took the mailing list and the billing list. Without those lists they could produce the magazine but didn't know who in the hell to send it to.

Now, the only thing I had to worry about was that Federal Warrant for my arrest. The cops stop looking at the city limits but the government never stops until they get to the border.

I remember driving down to N'awlins with Rose that night listening to Golden Earring's "Radar Love." The lyrics came alive "I've been driving all night, my hand's wet on the wheel...and its half past four and I'm shifting gear...no more speed I'm almost there..." I wasn't in love with Rose but I was deeply in like with her. I just knew this was going to be a great time for both of us.

Rose and I found a house that was converted into two apartments, we had the first floor. It was in the downtown area. Our first day in the new home we met a neighbor named Ted who lived across the street. He seemed like a nice enough guy who booked bands for a living.

I was working the graveyard shift although I didn't do that shift very long. We had only been in N'awlins for a couple of weeks. I still hadn't talked to any friends or family since we arrived except for my mother and that was from a pay phone miles from the house. I gave her my address in case of an emergency and told her not to write to me unless it was an extreme emergency, as in a death. I also told her we had no phone. We did, but it was in the landlord's name. I felt like we were in a gangster movie with all the precautions we had to take. It seemed weird since I really hadn't broken any laws. There was money to cover the check when I wrote it. It was the bank that screwed everything up.

I woke up about two o'clock one afternoon. Rose and I were sitting out on the porch drinking coffee when the mailman came walking up the driveway. He had a letter in his hand and it didn't look like junk mail. I could only hope it was for the former tenants. No such luck. As he handed it to me he asked "Does the 'M' stand for Mitch?" Not Mitchell mind you, but Mitch. That wasn't good I thought as I replied "No, Michael." As I looked at the letter, it was from Mother and it was addressed to R. M. McCracken. I told her not to write to me, DAMN her. Why would the mailman ask me about my name if they weren't on to me?

Rose and I rushed into the house as soon as he left.

Chapter 11: Going Down

We stood on our knees on the couch looking out the window. If we had guns we would have grabbed them at that point. I wanted to get the mattress off the bed to use it as a shield like Buck Barrow did in *Bonnie and Clyde*. My heart was pounding out of my chest. I had never been arrested or even in trouble with the law before. We watched out the window for hours and finally decided we were just being paranoid.

I found out later the mailman asked a neighbor what I did for a living. He was told that I was a DJ at WRNO doing graveyards. All those precautions and I used my real name on the air. Ego will get you every time. I was arrested the next day.

I was drug out of my home to an unmarked car. I was taken to the Postal Inspector's office where I was handcuffed to a chair. The Inspector was sitting backwards in a wooden chair, his arms crossed and resting on the back of it like Elliott Ness. He was smoking a cigarette, just holding it between his lips. The ashes were just about to drop. He squinted his eye and it was twitching as the cigarette smoke rose into his face. He was hacking, not a cough really but I could tell he wasn't used to it. This was all a tough guy act.

It was all I could do to not laugh out loud but I guess I had a grin on my face. "You think this is funny hippie boy?" he asked. With a chuckle I said "You got the wrong guy" playing along with his tough guy routine. He may have seen himself as Elliott Ness all I saw was

Barney Fife. He had Barney's interrogation skills.

He showed me the check. It was in a clear plastic evidence envelope. "Is that your signature?"

"Yes it is"

"You knew you didn't have funds in that account when you wrote that check now didn't ya?"

"Actually, I did have money in the account when I wrote the check."

"C'mon Mitch, I go to the grocery store every Wednesday night to buy groceries. I write a check that I know won't be good until Friday when I deposit my paycheck."

"You do that?"

"Of course I do, everybody does that. That's what you did too didn't ya Mitch?"

"No, like I said I had money in my account." I was young but I wasn't stupid, he was trying to get me to admit I broke the law. I looked him right in the eye and innocently asked "Isn't what you did at the grocery store called check fraud?"

"You DO think this is funny don't cha?"

Chapter 11: Going Down

"Just call the Attorney General in Memphis. His name's Hugh Stanton. I'm helping him with his investigation into the bank. He'll tell you my account was frozen after I wrote that check."

He looked at one of the other two men in the room. The ones who arrested me and said get "Mr. Stanton on the phone." Then he looked at me with that squint and warned "If he doesn't verify your story you'll be spending the night with us tonight." I just smiled and told him "If you're trying to intimidate me, it's gonna take more than a cigarette, rolled up sleeves and a sleepover invitation." These guys weren't cops, they were wannabe cops. This was probably the most excitement they'd had in years. I wasn't worried because I knew I didn't break any laws.

Mr. Stanton told his investigator that he would have the FBI Special Agent in charge of the investigation call within fifteen minutes, then he asked to speak to me. They put him on the speaker phone. "Joe Harwell and Al Bell will be indicted for embezzling 18.9 million dollars from small businessmen in Memphis. We would have got them eventually but without your tip, it would have taken a lot longer." I just smirked, shook my head and looked at Steve McGarrett and said "looks like Danno won't be booking me tonight as he started to stumble as he dismounted his chair. He was a little less smug now as his big bust was quickly turning into one more big Barney Fife fiasco. I died laughing and said "Nip it Ange, nip it right in the bud."

After the agent called I was released and driven back home. The charges were dropped. Joe Harwell and Al Bell were both indicted and that's all I knew for years. I hated them both for what they did to me, my staff of Memphis Music professionals and the Magazine.

It was years later before I found out that Al Bell was also claiming to be a victim of Joe Harwell. Al Bell was acquitted when Harwell admitted to forging his signature on the loan documents. A lot of people including me believed Al Bell was just as guilty as Joe Harwell. But consider this: When Harwell and Bell were indicted Joe Harwell was serving a five year term in Springfield, Illinois for embezzling $248,000 from the bank. He was issuing loans and checking accounts to fictitious persons. On the other hand, what could the bank do with the magazine? Stax HAD to be involved to benefit from the ownership of a magazine that rated records. In order for that to happen wouldn't Al Bell have to be in the loop?

According to court documents filed September 19, 1978: *In time, the bank relied upon Harwell as their music industry expert. Sizeable loan transactions were involved to record houses and affiliates. Primarily, these loans were handled by Harwell. He authorized loans for Stax Records from Union Planters in return he received cash payments from Stax. To Harwell the "Memphis Sound" became the source of pleasant and lucrative vibrations.*

In addition to that, Stax was ordered shut down by Federal Bank Judge William B. Leffler in early 1978. The

Chapter 11: Going Down

petition was filed by Union Planters Bank. At the time, they had no choice but to foreclose on Stax for more than 10.5 million dollars. That was a direct result of the loans, real and fictitious set up by Joe Harwell.

The really sad part of the Stax decline is that Jim Stewart had stepped back in and mortgaged his Memphis mansion to provide the label with short term working capital. When Judge Leffler ordered Stax shut down, Jim Stewart lost his home as a result.

The distribution deal with CBS records hurt Stax because once Clive Davis left CBS, the label lost interest in Stax. Still, they refused to let them out of their contract for fear they could get a deal with another label and become direct competition. Stax's profits were also cut severely when CBS refused to distribute to the small mom and pop record sellers in the black community which had been the backbone of Stax's record sales. They also weren't pushing the Stax product to the larger retailers for fear of undercutting rack space for CBS R&B artists like Sly and the Family Stone, Earth Wind and Fire and the Isley Brothers.

So while it's true the CBS deal wasn't good for and indeed hurt Stax. It was only a complication. The cause of Stax Records' death was simply Joe Harwell, his greed and his lack of ethics. He was supposed to be the bank's expert on Memphis music, instead he almost destroyed it. Al Bell will tell you he did the best he could to keep Stax alive. Harwell put a knife in Al Bell's back, killing

Stax and critically wounding Memphis Music.

Stax was gone and Memphis music has never regained the glory that it had at the height of Stax's popularity. Ardent Studios continues to bring in major artists to Memphis to record as well as some of the other studios but it's nothing like its heyday.

The Memphis music community continues to strive to regain its influence and leadership in the world of music. It's so much harder to make a comeback than it is to just make it, a comeback that wouldn't be necessary had it not been for one man, Joe Harwell.

As John Lennon said, "Instant Karma's gonna get you, gonna knock you right on the head." Joe Harwell only served two years for what he did to Stax and Memphis Music. But like OJ Simpson, his karma got him. He went from rubbing shoulders with Memphis music elite to being cellmates with big bubba. Joe Harwell did not get what he deserved, he deserved so much more. The Karma Court's decision is still out on Al Bell.

Chapter Twelve:
The City Of New Orleans

The time I spent in N'awlins was the best radio years of my career. It was fun once I got the check fraud charges dropped. That was a little stressful. Things lightened up after that. Well for a little while anyway. They were about to get heavy between Rose and me.

I came home one morning and found Rose sitting in bed soaking wet from head to toe and she was crying her heart out. "What the hell happened" I asked. She just pointed at the ceiling. As I looked up I saw what seemed to be a two by three foot hole in the ceiling still dripping water. It seems the lady who lived upstairs had fallen to sleep while running her bathwater. Her tub overflowed and the ceiling had given way.

"Well, why didn't you just go get a towel?" Rose started crying even harder and pointed to the bathroom. I walked over and turned on the light, there were about fifteen big black giant cock roaches scampering around. They were not like anything I've ever seen before they were Roachzillas. I tried to step on one of them and it was off to the races, it was like roller skating. We stayed the month and then moved about two blocks away.

I was starting to feel some distance between me and Rose. The closeness I had once felt was slipping away. I didn't know what it was just something in the way she was acting. Has anyone ever told you that if you are with someone who cheated to be with you will also cheat on you? Was Rose looking for greener pastures like when she wanted to get out of her relationship with her fiancé when we met? Hello? Duh!

One afternoon Rose said "We need to talk; I have something serious I want to talk to you about." Is that ever good news? Seems our friend Ted from across the street had taken Rose to a clinic the day before to abort our child. She never told me she was even pregnant. I was shocked and hurt. A lot of questions went through my head. Boy or girl? Why my opinion wasn't even considered? What if I wanted the child? Ever consider that? Wasn't it also mine? This would have been my first child, how could she do that?

I was single again. Rose and I split up. After she murdered my child, I handed her a pillow and pointed to the curb. She moved to Memphis with her fiancé, New Orleans with me and I understand she then moved to San Francisco with my neighbor from across the street. NEXT!

I moved back to the Causeway Hotel, where WRNO was. Half the building was a residential hotel. I was close to work, knew everyone that worked there. It had a good restaurant on the bottom floor and a bar on the top. Sounds like home to me. I had a new crop of beautiful women out at the pool every weekend and my own apt to take them to. This single thing is not so bad. Did I mention that DJ's have an equivalent to groupies called "hit line chicks?" Some women want to date you just because you are on the radio. It doesn't matter what you

Chapter 12: The City of New Orleans

look like.

I had become good friends with the office manager at WRNO. She was a very attractive Polynesian woman named Aloma and oddly enough she was from Houma, Louisiana. That's right Aloma from Houma. Swear ta God. She was married to a cop named Tommy, a nice guy for a cop. But just the same I didn't want them just poppin' in at my apartment if you know what I mean. Aloma was really a cool woman with two little girls about seven and five. She liked me too I'm sure because she introduced me to her beautiful niece, Miranka.

Miranka had also just ended a bad relationship, we didn't date as much as just hang out together. We went out drinking and dancing, we even went to some concerts together. Miranka was always fun. She liked to cut up as much as I did. Golden Earring was going to open for the Doobie Brothers at the Warehouse down on Tchoupitoulas Street, which was the main venue for rock music in the seventies. I asked Miranka to go with me. "Radar Love" had kind of been a special song for Rose and me. I knew Miranka would keep my mind off that. This romanticist thing isn't all it's cracked up to be, sometimes it's a bitch. When the relationship is going good it's great, but when it goes south it hurts like hell. I was on a roll being dumped by Marty and Pat and then Rose and her abortion. I was beginning to think it was me, nah that couldn't be it, must be the three of them.

The Warehouse had a great cook backstage that made

red beans and rice for every group that played there. Miranka and I were eating when Golden Earring came backstage and started to fill their plates. In N'awlins red beans and rice is a plate dish, not a bowl. Miranka had a great sense of humor and like me, enjoyed a good practical joke. I was unaware that Miranka spoke Dutch. Golden Earring is from the Netherlands. She walked over to the group's manager and started talking to him in Dutch and he immediately freaked out. He started running around backstage like a chicken with his head cut off. He yelled something at George and Rinus then he put his face in his hands and was on the verge of tears. George and Rinus looked over at Miranka in amazement and their collective jaws dropped. I looked at her and asked "what the hell did you say to him?" She could hardly talk, she was laughing so hard. She said "I told him I was from the Netherlands and had stowed away on their flight over. Some of the roadies had hidden me at all the other shows, but now I'm homesick and I want to go back to the Netherlands."

George and Rinus where still watching us and saw how hard we were laughing and started to shake their heads no as we did the same to let them know she was kidding. They died laughing. The manager looked up from his hands and very slowly started to laugh although he didn't know why until we told him he had been Punk'd years before Ashton Kutcher was even born. They were very forgiving and hung out with us for the rest of the night. It seems she spoke Dutch to Barry Hay and he put her up to it. Good Times in N'awlins. A

Chapter 12: The City of New Orleans

practical joke is a great ice breaker to get to know some of the groups. They get tired of people kissing up to them and seem to enjoy it when you have the balls to mess with them.

Rose was out and Miranka was in. I was made the Music Director at WRNO and life was good. One of the first songs I added was Neil Sedaka's "Laughter in the Rain". Within a week The MCA Promotion Man, Rick Rockhill came into my office and handed me a New York phone number and asked me to call it. Neil wanted to personally thank me for adding the song. It was not yet on the national charts but I knew it would be. How cool is that? I get to talk to rock and roll icon, Neil Sedaka.

I called the number and a lady answered the phone. "May I speak to Neil Sedaka please?"

"May I tell him who's calling?"

"Sure, this is Mitch McCracken in New Orleans." She said "This is Neil"...his voice was so high I thought it was a woman, of course I didn't tell him that. But I guess I just did. We talked a few minutes and he told me he had left the states and moved to London years earlier because of the violence here. He was playing in a club In London when Elton John saw him and signed him to his Rocket Label, distributed here in the states by MCA.

He went on to say the same album across the pond was a greatest hits album. Then he had to go pick the kids up from school. I thought that was cool, just a regular dad with a golden voice.

The Captain and Tennille had a hit with a cover of his "Love will Keep Us Together" from the same album. At the end of the song as it begins to fade you can hear Toni Tennille say "Sedaka's Back," the name of the album here.

To promote the album he briefly opened for the Carpenters. He was kicked off the tour because he was getting a better reception than the headliners. Trivia fact: the drummer for the Carpenter's tour was the Mickey Mouse Club's Cubby O'Brien.

Radio was still fun then and I was having a great time. I went to a lot of concerts but by far the best concert I saw in New Orleans was a new artist from New Jersey named Bruce Springsteen and his E Street Band. It was the summer of '75, just before Born to Run was released. I saw Bruce at the Performing Arts Centre in New Orleans.

At one point, as he was introducing "The E Street Shuffle" and was talking about how he met the band

Chapter 12: The City of New Orleans

members in the E Street Band. He said he was walking through an alley in New Jersey. It got dark at the end of the alley. As he approached he saw why. There was a gigantic black man standing at the end of the alley. Bruce said he pulled out his wallet and threw it at the man's feet and said "Don't hurt me." The man said "No Mr. Bruce I wants to be in your band." It was of course "the big man" Clarence Clemmons and they broke into the song.

We were playing songs from both the first two albums *Greetings from Asbury Park New Jersey* and *The Wild, the Innocent and the E Street Shuffle* at WRNO. They played so many great songs that night like "Spirit in the Night", "Kitty's Back", "Rosalita" and "4th July Asbury Park (Sandy)". They also did songs from the new album including the title, "Jungleland", "Thunder Road" and "10th Avenue Freeze Out".

It was the first time since the Beatles that I felt so strongly about a group. I was so moved by what I saw that night that I called my brother Ronnie and told him I had just seen a group that was going to be the biggest thing since the Beatles. In many ways they were, the power of Born to Run also got the first two albums on the national charts. But I think Jon Landau put it best when he said "I have seen the future of rock 'n' roll and its name is Bruce Springsteen."

WRNO somehow got a hold of a bootleg song by Bruce called "The Fever". It was a great song and one of the best vocals I ever heard Bruce do. Freddy, the local Columbia promotion man asked us to lose it. Bruce never released it but Southside Johnny & the Asbury Jukes did on their I *Don't Want to Go Home* album. I talked about that show for weeks.

I didn't get to meet Springsteen but I did have the pleasure of meeting a member of the group I compared him to, Paul McCartney. In 1975 McCartney came to town to do some recording. He recorded much of his *Venus and Mars* album at Allen Toussaint's Sea-Saint studios with the studio house band, the Meters. During Mardi Gras he rented a German restaurant on the parade route.

I was in a bar drinking and having a great time. That's easy to do while Mardi Gras is going on. All of a sudden Paul and Linda McCartney came in unannounced. They were there for a couple of hours. He bought rounds for the house several times and talked a few minutes with everyone there. Linda was sitting at a table as Paul went around the bar talking to everyone and seemed to be in the Mardi Gras spirit. I just got a minute with him. I asked how many songs he actually wrote with John Lennon he smiled and said "Very few." Lennon went into more depth about that in the book Lennon Remembers and his song "How Do You Sleep" from his album *Imagine*.

McCartney was so kind and genuine. Not what I expected at all. Although I just talked to him briefly he

Chapter 12: The City of New Orleans

struck me as a very down to earth guy.

Here's another bar story for you. One night after dinner I headed to the bar on the top floor of the Causeway Hotel. At the time I had brown hair that I wore in a ponytail, a slight receding hair line and I had a beard.

After a couple of drinks a man came up and sat next to me at the bar. A few minutes later he leaned towards me almost touching shoulders and in a whisper he asked "You're George Carlin aren't you?" I kind of laughed and said "No, I wish". How cool is that, the guy thinks that I'm the hippest comedian in the world. I thought to myself do I look that much like Carlin? Nah not really, it's just the beard and ponytail. He wouldn't let it go. He said "it's ok, I won't tell anyone, you can tell me." No matter what I said he wouldn't believe that I wasn't George Carlin. I explained to him my name's Mitch McCracken and I'm a DJ at WRNO. "Can I buy you a drink" he wanted to know. I said "ok, but you have to understand I'm not George Carlin." He just gave me a grin and a wink and said "Whatever you say, George". He bought me drinks for the week or so that he was in town. Every night we had the same discussion and I kept telling him "I'm not George Carlin."

Finally he told me he was leaving the next day. I was relieved I was so tired of him thinking I was someone else. When he left the hotel I felt better because I wouldn't have that ongoing debate to convince him that

I'm Not George Carlin.

The night after he left I was relaxing at the bar, sipping on my Margarita (straight up on the rocks with salt, not the frozen sissy drink). I was feeling a lot better because the debate was now over. I took a deep breath, leaned back and looked around to see if there were any good looking women in the bar to impress with my celebrity. Hey, you use what you have, I'm not good looking or built very well, kind of thin at the time so I had to use my humor and mediocre fame. As I was looking around an older tourist couple walked in. They came over to the bar. "Hey, how ya doin" I asked as he pulled her stool out for her. "Great, how are you" as he took a seat beside me, when he did he gave me a pat on the shoulder and said "What 'cha drinkin' Mr. Carlin?" I was flabbergasted, "What did you call me?" I demanded. "Oh, a guy who was in here last night told me who you were," here we go again. As I started the "I'm not George Carlin" speech ...this went on for six months or so. Finally someone didn't spread the word but at one point everyone in the bar knew me as George. I was like Norm on Cheers "where everyone knows your name" only they didn't know my real name. I realized why celebrities never run out of money, because they never have to spend it.

It was a very sad day when I heard that George Carlin died. It was like a piece of me had died too. He had one of the greatest comedic minds of his or any other generation. His thing was words and he mastered them,

Chapter 12: The City of New Orleans

even some you can't say on the radio. I saw an interview he did with Matt Lauer on the Today Show. Carlin said he would determine where the line was on a topic and deliberately step over it and he stepped over it often.

I had always been a fan going back to his days on the Ed Sullivan show and The Tonight Show. I was first drawn to him when I was just dreaming of being a disc jockey. He was on TV doing "Wonderful WINO", a bit he used to do about a DJ at a fictional radio station. I felt a close bond with him after being mistaken for him. I saw him several times when I lived in Las Vegas. Never thought that I looked like him at all but I loved what he did and how he did it.

Just after I cut the ponytail off

Radio Daze

When he did "The 7 Words You Can't Say on the Radio", there wasn't really a FCC ruling against those seven words. That's until some idiot in New York played the bit on the radio. A man was listening with his young son in the car. He filed a complaint with the FCC and before you know it there was a ruling passed by the Supreme Court against those seven words. Amazing isn't it, life imitating art.

Chapter Thirteen:
The Pretender

I have seen some great concerts in my lifetime. I saw, Jimi Hendrix open for the Monkees, the Who perform the Rock Opera's Tommy and Quadrophenia, Emerson, Lake and Palmer's Trilogy tour, Leon Russell and the Shelter People, Mountain, Grand Funk, Black Sabbath, Elton John's first American tour and many, many more great shows but I would have to say seeing the Doors in New Orleans was the most disappointing and depressing show I've ever witnessed, just beating out Joe Cocker's vomit tour.

Being in radio for all these years I have found that nobody calls the station when they like the song, they wait and call when they think the song sucks. So I like to be as positive as I can but it's impossible to be positive about that show. It was at the Warehouse, which was where Beaver Productions did all their New Orleans shows at the time. I was just about six months away from my first radio job. This was a $5 concert. Unbelievable, the Doors for five bucks. I loved the Doors' music as everyone did at that time and I was looking forward to hearing their songs like "Love Me Two Times," "Hello, I Love You," "People Are Strange," etc. They had just released "Absolutely Live" a couple of months before and I wanted to see them do "Celebration of the Lizard." The part where Morrison screams "WAKE UP" would later knock me off my chair when I played it for the first time on the air (I was stoned, my eyes were closed with the headphones turned up). We were going to see one of the greatest groups in the world, but what we saw was a

Radio Daze

live Public Service Announcement for drug and alcohol abuse.

There wasn't a high point to this show (no pun intended) Morrison was in bad shape, I don't know if it was drugs or alcohol or a combination of the two. Some thought it was a mental breakdown but I thought that was a little over the top. He was milling around the stage telling bad jokes and mumbling what lyrics he could

Chapter 13: The Pretender

remember which wasn't a lot. I don't recall how many songs they attempted that night but I do remember the last song that Morrison tried to sing was "Light My Fire." He kept slamming the microphone on the floor in frustration I assume because he couldn't remember the lyrics. He finally stopped singing and stumbled over to John Densmore and just slumped down, sitting in front of the drum set. He was unable to stand up, so the rest of the group jammed for a few minutes and then Densmore tried to push him back up to his feet with his foot. Morrison was unable to finish the show and left the stage. We were all in shock. We knew it wasn't an act. What had we just witnessed? The rest of the band walked off the stage for the last time as the Doors.

Morrison died a few months later on July 3, 1971 in Paris. I had no trouble believing it was a drug overdose even though the official cause of death was a heart attack. At 27 years old? He was the third major rock star to die of a drug overdose in less than a year. Jimi Hendrix died on September 18, 1970 and Janis Joplin passed away about two weeks later on October 4th. Oddly enough they were all 27 at the time of their death.

There have been stories lately about Jim Morrison still being alive and it reminded me of a time that seems so long ago and yet just like yesterday. It was in New Orleans back in 1974 just three years after Morrison's Death. I was filling in on the Midday shift at WRNO in New Orleans. As it turned out Joe was a real easy man to work for, just like I thought he would be. He knew what direction he wanted the station to go in. The problem was although he knew where he wanted to go. He didn't necessarily know how to get there. He was a great guy and even though he owned the station he was very open minded. If you had a different opinion than his, he would at least hear you out. If you had enough logic you could talk him into almost anything.

One day he walked into the control room with a big smile on his face. He said "You'll never guess who's out in the lobby!" He was like a big kid sometimes when he was excited about something. I just looked at him for a minute as he stared at me with that big goofy smile frozen on his face. He REALLY wanted me to guess. "Okay" I said finally "So tell me." He looked at me like a kid on Christmas morning and said "Jim Morrison of the Doors that's who." I could tell he really believed it so I fought hard to hold back my grin. "I want you to interview him right now." I knew I had to bust his bubble. Back then disc jockeys had some say as to what was played and who was interviewed during their shift. I had to think of my credibility. Everyone knew Morrison was dead. Ok, so there were some questions. But this guy whoever he was wouldn't have the answers. I tried to play it down by asking Joe if the rigor mortis was very bad. He didn't laugh. "Look Joe, Jim Morrison is dead. He died in Paris three years ago. I don't know who this guy is but I don't want to give him air time on my shift." I could see his chins start to quiver as the anger started to surface "If you don't interview him...your replacement will." I knew Joe well enough to know he wasn't going to

Chapter 13: The Pretender

give in on this one.

This guy had sold Joe on the fact that he's the real Jim Morrison. Joe saw this as a worldwide exclusive. I had to think of some way of saving myself. I couldn't come across as if I believed this was really Jim Morrison. I told Joe "Okay, but if this guy turns out to be an imposter it's on you, not me. Just give me a few minutes before bringing Jim back for the interview." I got everything ready that I thought I would need for the Media event of the year.

When Joe brought "Jim" back to the control room I was shocked because he was overweight, walked with a cane and had very feminine mannerisms. He looked like a bad picture of Jim Morrison on the back of the Doors 13 album. He did have a California Drivers License with Jim Morrison's name on it (James Douglas Morrison) and was sitting on ready to show it to me. It seemed to me that he was gay, not that there's anything wrong with that, I just knew that Morrison wasn't. I have always been a big fan of the Doors and I couldn't let this buffoon get away with the hoax that he was Jim Morrison. Jim Morrison was cool, hip and could grow a beard overnight it seemed. This guy was fat, ugly and anything but cool or hip. We talked for a few minutes before going on the air. He may have been able to fool someone who never saw the Doors but when Jim Morrison was in a room, he owned it. I never let on that I thought he was a fraud. The song ended and we went on the air.

"RNO I'm Mitch and that's Eric Clapton with "Motherless Children" from RNO's feature album *461 Ocean Boulevard*, We have a special guest with us this morning. I think most of you remember Jim Morrison of the Doors. Jim tells me that the rumors of his death are a bit premature. So tell me Jim, what happened in Paris?"

"Well Mitch, it wasn't me but my double that died."

"Oh you had a double?"

"Yeah, my management company had a guy who looked and sounded like me. I was doing a lot of morphine at the time and didn't always make it to the shows. So my double would fill in for me. Anyway he died and I took the opportunity to go underground."

"So you're telling me that they had a guy who looked like you, sounded like you and was more dependable than you?

"Well yeah, as bad as that sounds, that's right."

I started to turn the heat up a bit to see what his reaction would be. I looked him right in the eye and asked "So tell me Jim, what did they need with you?" His demeanor turned from pleasant to shock. He was insulted and got a little defensive. The real Jim Morrison would never allow a question like that. His attitude from what I knew about him, would have been I don't care if you believe me or not and left. The imposter on the other

Chapter 13: The Pretender

hand was making excuses. He tried to explain it away by saying "Hey, I'm a song writer."

Well, so is Neil Sedaka." He just looked at me with nowhere to go. I don't think Jim Morrison would ever be speechless. After a few seconds as I rolled the record I cued up when Joe went to get him and said "Well I'll tell ya what Jim, I've got "Riders on the Storm" cued up on the turntable, why don't you sing along?"

As he struggled with his cane to get up, he said "I didn't come here to do a concert."

"It's one song, that's hardly a concert. This will remove any doubt as to if you are really Jim Morrison. It will prove you are Jim Morrison, or you are *not* Jim Morrison."

"I'm NOT singing."

"Well then, I would have to say that you are NOT Jim Morrison."

As the vocal of the song approaches "Jim" finally limps out of the control room. As the door squeaks open I said "So I guess your double would have come in handy today uh, Jim?" The door shut behind him and I just let the record play, turned off the mic and sat back in my chair with a smile and a sense of satisfaction for exposing him as the imposter he was. He had other interviews scheduled around town. They were all cancelled.

Radio Daze

Billboard Magazine ran a story about that interview, the imposter claiming to be Jim Morrison and the disc jockey who exposed him on the air. Joe was furious with me the day it happened but later he was thankful that we were the station that put a stop to Jim Morrison's big comeback. That could have been very embarrassing for the station, but luckily I wasn't as gullible as Joe. How could he think that he could pull that off without having to sing?

About a year later after I left the station, I was looking for work. I saw an ad in the paper for a manager of a record shop in the French Quarter about a block from where I lived. The only problem was the interview would have to take place in Baton Rouge. So I drove up to do the interview with a man named Billy Casselberry. I walked into Mr. Casselberry's office and as he looked up I said "Before you ask me any questions, I have one for you, it's about the job." He smiled and said "Sure." "Its Jim isn't it" I asked. He just looked down and said "to some people." I smiled and said "Well you can stop the interviewing now, I got this job" and I did.

He had written a book by then as Jim Morrison called The Bank of America of Louisiana and was trading the throw-away book for records (even trade) through All South Distributors. All South distributed records and books, so he was getting records for about 35 cents. That's what it cost to print the book. His family owned a printing company. He decided instead of just underselling everybody else, he would sell single albums for $1.00 and doubles for $2.00. At the time single disc

Chapter 13: The Pretender

albums were selling for around $6.00. So not only was he a liar and a fraud he was also a bad businessman. The record store he called Zeppelin Records, giving the impression there was some connection to the group Led Zeppelin. The records were selling but the book wasn't. So once he established the record prices and he sold the opening inventory he was in trouble. When the record shop folded he owed me two weeks pay. The law in the state of Louisiana at the time was if you go out of business, you have to pay your employees right then. If you don't they stay on the payroll until you do. I won a judgment for $3,400. I have yet to receive a dime from that judgment. He OJ'ed me. Billy Casselberry was later sentenced to prison for fraud and embezzlement not related to the late Jim Morrison.

That was one of the shortest and yet most satisfying interviews I ever did. Jim Morrison had gone downhill the last year or so of his life but he deserved respect and I refused to let this idiot take that away from him.

Chapter Fourteen:
Free Bird

Lynyrd Skynyrd is one of my favorite groups and have been from the first time I heard them when they opened for the Who's Quadrophenia tour back in '73.

One of my best friends, Rick Rockhill was the MCA promotion man that covered New Orleans back in the mid 70's. He had just heard that Skynyrd was going to be nearby as part of what was later called "the Torture Tour." They were going to be in Hattiesburg, MS. The show was in March of 1975. I had a vacation coming up and I was talking to Rick about what to do and where to go. He suggested I at least go to Hattiesburg to see them. Skynyrd would also be coming to New Orleans a little later with the same tour. That was just too cool, going on the road with Lynyrd Skynyrd, hell yeah!

The tour was promoting their *Nuthin' Fancy* album. That night in Hattiesburg, I went to watch an interview at a little station there. The call letters were WXXX. Talk about a small station with no budget at all. It was in a building that was made out of tin with rickety floors, thin hallways and even thinner walls. I walked into the control room and the mics didn't have wind screens on them. Well, they did but it was the foam rubber from the arm of a couch. I'm talking about a big rectangle chunk of foam rubber stuck onto the microphone. The band did the interview. Ronnie didn't go for some reason. As soon as it was over we headed to the venue for the show. I rode with Rick and on the way he said "Look Mitch I know you, and I know you like to joke around but these guys get into a fight at the drop of a hat." I knew that could happen, Skynyrd was known to get into fights on stage from time to time. Rick made his point by asking "So no kidding around tonight right?"

Just then we pulled up to the venue, it was at Reed Green Coliseum on the campus of the University of Southern Miss. It looked a little bigger than a high school auditorium I never did answer his question and for a good reason. How often do you get to meet members of a group as hot as they were at that time? If you're going to meet them, you have to make an impression, right? I remembered how much other bands like Golden Earring liked it when I messed with them instead of patronizing them. I didn't want to just meet Ronnie Van Zant, I wanted to get to know him.

We went backstage to meet the band. It was the first tour with Artimus Pyle who had replaced Bob Burns as the drummer. Ed King was still with them, he was the first one I met. We talked a little about Skynyrd but mostly about Strawberry Alarm Clock. He was the guitarist when they recorded "Incense and Peppermints" which went to #1 on the charts back in '67. The Alarm Clock went through some changes and Ed ended up playing bass. He told me that while he was touring, Skynyrd opened for them. Skynyrd didn't even have a record deal then but Ed could see that they would soon. He told Ronnie that if they ever needed another guitar player he would like to play with them.

Chapter 14: Free Bird

When Leon Wilkeson quit the band, Van Zant called and asked Ed about playing bass. King joined the band as Wilkeson's replacement. It was cool hearing rock history being told by someone who had lived it. Ed told me that before the release of the first album, Van Zant took him aside and told him he was the worst bass player he had ever worked with. Ed said he thought he was out of the band, but Van Zant just wanted him to switch to guitar.

Ronnie was able to get Wilkeson to rejoin the band. Ed co-wrote "Sweet Home Alabama" with Ronnie and Gary Rossington. It is Ed that does the countdown at the beginning of the song as well as the opening guitar licks. As happy as he sounded that night to be a part of Lynyrd Skynyrd, it was hard to believe that in a little more than two months he would just walk away. But that's just what he did on May 26th, 1975.

I also talked to Artimus Pyle who had just returned from the service maybe a year or two before. He said he was loving the tour, he said it was much better than his last tour – as a marine in Viet Nam.

I was talking to Ed and Artimus in the dressing room when Rick walked in with Ronnie Van Zant. He brought him over to me and started to introduce us when I butted in "Yeah, Ronnie and I know each other." Rick just looked at me and shook his head. Ronnie looked a little puzzled and said "I don't know you man."

"C'mon Ronnie, it's me Mitch, Mitch McCracken." I could see he was trying to place me. He didn't want to insult me. I was the Music Director at a station in a major market. The Music Director is the one who decides what's played on the air. Then he said "I'm sorry man I just don't know you." Not giving up I asked "You remember that song "Mississippi Kid about the model from Florence, Alabama?" He got a shocked look on his face and his mouth dropped. "How the hell did you know that?"

Chapter 14: Free Bird

"I can't believe this, really? You never met me before?" That was my story and I was sticking to it. "I'm sorry man, if I did meet you, I don't remember you" he said with a real sincere look on his face. I almost felt bad but I played it to the max. I had to act like I was highly pissed that this guy's so full of himself he doesn't remember the "little" people. I held my hand up, looked down, shook my head and said "Whatever Dude, you're not that famous" and with that I stormed off and headed to my 3rd row seats to watch the show. I knew I better get out of his way or I might get hit as Rick had predicted.

Grinderswitch was the opening act. They recorded for Capricorn Records but never had the following as some of the label's other artist like The Allman Brothers and the Marshall Tucker Band. I got a chance to talk to group member Paul Hornsby. I was already aware of him from playing in a group called the Hour Glass with Duane and Gregg Allman. We talked about a little about that group; he told me how they were discovered by the Nitty Gritty Dirt Band's manager Bill McEuen. There was a cut on their first album called the B.B. King Medley that was outstanding. They sounded just like B.B. between Duane's guitar work and Gregg's voice. It was also included on the Duane Allman Anthology album. Hornsby later became a producer with Capricorn and then as an independent. He produced albums for artists like the Charlie Daniels Band, the Marshall Tucker Band and Wet Willie. He also played with Elvin Bishop and Captain Beyond. Not to mention having a couple of hits on his own with his group Bruce Hornsby and the Range,

"Every Little Kiss" and "The Way it is."

The show was great. I knew this was a vacation I would remember for the rest of my life. The three guitarists, Allen Collins, Gary Rossington and Ed King were tearing it up. They sounded so good live. I couldn't believe that Ed was ever the Bass player after seeing him play guitar that night. Like everyone else I was waiting to hear them play the new concert anthem Free Bird. When they did they turned on the Disco Ball and the crowd went wild.

After the show we headed to the hotel, the Holiday Inn in beautiful downtown Hattiesburg. We were all down in the bar. I had a couple of shots of tequila and I have to tell you I'm a cheap date. I can take the top off a beer, put it in my mouth and get a buzz. I'm also a happy drunk and have been known to be attracted to the posts that hold up the ceiling. I was feeling pretty good when I noticed Van Zant was looking at me through the corner of my eye. I thought oh shit; here he comes, he's going to cold cock me now as he started towards me. I was still pretending to be highly insulted that he wouldn't remember a guy as memorable as me. I should also point out that Van Zant had given up drugs and hard liquor by that time. He was just drinking some wine. Otherwise Rick's prediction may have been right on target.

Van Zant walked up to me and said in an almost apologetic tone "You know man; you do look kind of familiar." I couldn't hold it in I just died laughing. Van

Chapter 14: Free Bird

Zant got this big grin on his face and said "I don't know you do I?" I admitted that he didn't know me, that we had never met. He said "Ok then, tell me how did you know who I wrote "Mississippi Kid" about?" "Well," I explained "I used to work for Sam Phillips at his station in Florence, WQLT. The model you wrote the song for has a little sister. She called me at the station and told me the story. I just took a shot that it could be true." He said it *was* true and then said "I could have kicked your ass for talking to me like that." "But cha didn't" I said with a laugh hoping to get him to laugh along with me. He did and we grabbed a table and started talking. I had done just what I set out to do and that was to get to know him, not just shake his hand.

We started talking about the history of the group and I impressed him even more with what I already knew about them. I knew that they got their name from their gym teacher Leonard Skinner, who went into Real Estate after they made him famous. The group started out as My Back Yard and they had been discovered by producer and one time member of The Blues Project, Al Kooper. He saw them in a club in Atlanta in '72. I was a big fan of Kooper too because he did a great album in '67 called Super Sessions. That album had a great version of Donovan's "Season of the Witch" that went on for about eleven minutes. Al Kooper was also the original lead singer of Blood, Sweat and Tears and sang "I Love You More Than You'll Ever Know."

"What else do you know about Al?" Ronnie asked me.

"I know that he wrote "This Diamond Ring" for the Drifters and when they turned it down Gary Lewis and the Playboys took to the top of the charts in 1964." I said with a grin. Ronnie was pretty impressed with what I knew and he realized how serious I was about their music.

We talked about other artist that influenced them like the Charlie Daniels Band, Marshall Tucker Band, Free, the Who and the Allman Brothers Band. Ronnie told me "You know, when Allen and I wrote "Free Bird" we never thought it would replace the Allman Brothers "Whipping Post" as the Southern Rock concert anthem. The strange thing" he said "is that the song's about Duane Allman."

Of all the people I've interviewed and met in my years in radio, and there have been many, Ronnie Van Zant was different. He was focused on the music and his career. He realized, right or wrong what he said and did influenced a lot of people and he was taking that more seriously than he had in the past.

I returned to New Orleans and to work at WRNO. A couple of weeks later the tour came to the Crescent City and Rick brought Skynyrd to the station. It was a Sunday and my day off but Ronnie had Rick call me and ask that I come up to the station to do the interview. Rick put Ronnie on the phone. I explained that when an artist comes by the station, whoever is on at that time does the interview. Granted the guy on the air was a part timer and that did deserve some consideration. Ronnie said "it

Chapter 14: Free Bird

isn't often that I can do an interview with someone I actually know"... "So you admit you know me now" I said cutting him off. We both started laughing and I told him I would be there in a few minutes.

I went up to the station and we were on the air together for six hours playing all the groups we had talked about the Allman Brothers Band, the Marshall Tucker Band, Charlie Daniels Band, Al Kooper and a little bit of Skynyrd. We would talk a while and play some music then talk a little more. He told me about what liquor and drugs had done to him, how it caused the on stage fights. He decided to slow down and get more serious about his music. He told me he and his wife Judy wanted to start a family so he started looking at things differently. He said he was writing a song about it. The song turned out to be "That Smell" that ended up on what would be his last album, *Street Survivors*. He even had me play some Neil Young solo stuff that day. Van Zant was a big fan and said he just had to give him a hard time about "Southern Man" in "Sweet Home Alabama."

I was right. I still remember that night in Hattiesburg like it was yesterday. By the time the plane went down in '77 I was back in my hometown working at Rock 103. I was doing 7-midnight. It had been announced that the plane had crashed and that three band members were dead, but hadn't said who they were. I knew that if Ronnie was dead, so was Skynyrd. As Artimus Pyle would later say "He was Lynyrd Skynyrd."They all wrote music, but Ronnie wrote almost all the lyrics and that's what gave the group its personality. I got off the air at midnight and stayed at the station until the announcement was made, as I recall around two Memphis time. Ronnie was dead. The other two members who died were from Memphis. Guitarist Steve Gains who had just been added as the third guitarist replacing Ed King and his sister, backup singer Cassie Gains. The man who had given me one of the most exciting nights of my life had also given me one of the saddest. There will never be another one like Ronnie Van Zant.

Chapter Fifteen
All the Young Girls Love Alice

I must admit that when Alice Cooper's first album came out they made me a little uncomfortable. I say they because for the first few albums Alice Cooper was the name of a group as well as its leader. I just had a problem with a guy calling himself Alice while wearing a tad bit too much makeup. I thought they would be a flash in the pan until I started really listening to the music. By their third album **Love it to Death** I thought they were damn good. They had a gimmick but they were also really good. Usually bands are one or the other.

In May of 1975 I found out that I was going to be interviewing Alice Cooper along with Gary Guthrie. But before I get to the interview I would like to first introduce you to Gary.

Gary was hired after I was and he had also worked at our competitor WNOE-FM. He went by the name Trigger Black there and at WRNO. When he worked at WNOE-AM he was Max Bozeaux. That's Max Bozo spelled Cajun style. Gary was so talented and creative; he surprised me every day with the things he came up with. I have found that you can be friends with almost anyone but the bond and friendship is so much greater when it's someone you admire and respect. To this day I feel as close to Gary as I did back in the 70's. He was bigger than life, never boring, he was always moving forward and growing creatively.

Gary always had a big smile on his face and had charisma like no one I've ever known. He was like a big blond teddy bear with a great disposition.

As far as radio programming, production and music rotation was concerned Gary was like a wide eyed kid in a candy store. He had an undying thirst for knowledge. He asked me to try to help him come up with our own format for album rock stations. I was more interested in living for the day and after my experience with the magazine I was more than happy to let someone else have the headaches for a while.

I was doing graveyards when Gary was hired, in fact I had called Jon Scott to tell him I was fed up with radio and was getting out for good. That, by the way was the fifth time I was getting out of radio for good. Jon wasn't there, but I told Rain (short for Lorraine), his wife what was going on. She said "Jon told me once that if anyone makes it in radio, it would be you." That was all I needed to hear, Jon effin Scott believed in me. I sucked it up and dealt with my problems.

Gary came up with a format and Joe appointed him the Program Director, now my best friend was my boss. That was kind of like having an alliance with the head of household. Gary moved me from the all night shift to 7-Midnight.

He called me into the control room one day while he was on the air and turned up the monitor nice and loud, it was ZZ Top from their Tres Hombres album. The song

Chapter 15: All the Young Girls Love Alice

was "La Grange." I looked at Gary with my arms outreached like Alfred E Newman as if to say "SO" and said "Heard the song before." With a smile he asked "Have you? Not like this, listen." When the vocal came around to my surprise it was in Spanish. Gary had a promotional Spanish version of the album and synchronized the English and Spanish versions. One on each turntable, during the music break he switched which one was on the air. So anyone listening heard English as normal and then the next verse was Spanish. That was really cool. He did the same thing with an instrumental version of "Sally G" the Paul McCartney song by Lloyd Green. He played the Wings version and when the vocal came back around it wasn't there because he switched songs. That was when radio was fun, when you were allowed to be creative. The listeners liked it better too because they never knew what to expect, it was exciting for them as well.

I took the ball and ran with it. I had just heard a comedy album by a group called the Credibility Gap which included Harry Shearer (Saturday Night Live, The Simpsons and a member of the fictitious group Spinal Tap), Michael McKean (Lenny on Laverne and Shirley and also a member Spinal Tap) and David L. Lander (who played Squiggy on Laverne and Shirley), they were great. They had a skit on the album doing a takeoff of the Tonight Show when Carson was king. They opened with the theme and Ed McMahon announcing who was going to be on that night. It sounded just like the real Tonight Show opening and they had Johnny Carson, Ed

Radio Daze

McMahon and Don Rickles down pat. I had a TV in the control room tuned to NBC. I was playing Mike Oldfield's "Tubular Bells" (Theme to The Exorcist) because it was an instrumental and I could dump it whenever I needed to. I kept watching and as soon as the tonight show came on I dumped the song and hit the Tonight Show track on the Credibility Gap album. The phone lit up with people calling in telling me how I flipped them out. They were listening to the radio and watching TV passing around a joint or bong and their worlds collided when the Tonight Show came on.

Another skit on the album was a public service film about sex education for high school students. You could actually hear the film dragging just like the movies we used to watch in school. The actors sounded like they were reading their lines too, it was so cheesy. At the end of the skit the teacher was talking about VD and said "this dry lifeless form on my desk was at one time a fourteen year old girl." When I got to the last ten or fifteen seconds or so I started my next record. I had the volume potted all the way down and slowly faded it up. As the skit concluded it was at full volume and you could hear the drums and then the vocal of Foghat's "I Just Want To Make Love To You." Those were the days.

Gary was from Kentucky and just married Becky, his longtime girlfriend from there while we were at WRNO. A few years later when the relationship started to get into trouble and fall apart he took it much further than the two turntable technique to let her know that he still cared for her.

Chapter 15: All the Young Girls Love Alice

Gary Guthrie when he was PD at WAKY

At the time he was the Program Director of WAKY in Louisville, his favorite station growing up. He went into the production studio with Neil Diamond's version of "You Don't Send Me Flowers." He put it on one turntable and he put Streisand's version on the other turntable. Then he went to work. He edited them until he had made a duet from them. It was beautiful. They sang the song in the same key. Streisand's tempo was a little slower so he had to alter that a little bit. It wasn't easy but he was determined to create the perfect parting gift for Becky, and he did. That's how their 1979 hit was born, from the WAKY mind of Gary Guthrie.

Before you knew it Gary was hearing from People magazine, the LA Times, Good Morning America, Merv Griffin, Casey Kasem, even the Aussie version of Johnny Carson wanted to hear the story. His fifteen minutes of fame that he was destined to achieve had indeed arrived. Now he's the answer (or is it a question) on "Jeopardy!"

So now you know who I was working with on that interview and honestly Gary did most of the interview. I was there for moral support and to fill in gaps if there were any. Still, that was a great interview. It really surprised me. I thought I knew what to expect from Alice, but I was wrong. It was also strange in the fact that it was a phone interview. Alice was in Nashville about to do a show there and we were in New Orleans at WRNO. Joe was out of town so he wanted the interview on tape (reel to reel in those days) because he too thought he knew what to expect from Alice. He was worried of what

Chapter 15: All the Young Girls Love Alice

Alice might say and wanted us to use a delay. We didn't, but we should have. We called the hotel in Nashville where Alice was staying, rolled the tape and waited for Alice to answer.

"Hello"

"Hi. Alice?"

"Nah man this is Fat Frankie, I'm Alice's bodyguard and I'm the Baddest Mother Fucker..."

"Hi Frank, you're live on the air!"

"Here's Alice"
(Edit, Edit, Edit)

Remember, we were recording for the owner of the station and didn't use the delay as we were told. So we had to go back, edit it and then dub it onto another reel of tape so Joe wouldn't see the splice. At the time of the interview "Only Women Bleed" had just hit the airwaves. Now here's a guy that sang "I Love the Dead," "Dead Babies" and "Muscle of Love." Before we even listened to the song, we just looked at the title and thought this can't be good. Should we even play this song?

The first thing that we asked Alice was about that song. It was from his first solo album *Welcome to my Nightmare*. The success of the album as it turned out, was that single. The song was still very controversial. The re-

Radio Daze

cord company, Atlantic initially shortened the title to "Only Women." The single was protested by some feminist groups claiming it was sexist and insulting. Those offended by the lyrics, missed the point of the song.

Alice said "I knew that the song would get that reaction initially. The song was about a victim of abuse (he quoted some of the lines in the song) She spends her life through pleasing up her man. He slaps her once in awhile and she lives and loves the pain." Alice went on "It's bad enough that she was in the relationship, but what makes it worse is that she stayed in it."

This is not the Alice Cooper I thought we would be interviewing, what really impressed me about him was

Chapter 15: All the Young Girls Love Alice

how intelligent he was. It wasn't about snakes, dressing in drag or wearing makeup. He had sympathy for the character and was willing to acknowledge the situation was tragic. That just blew me away; Alice was becoming less of an icon and more of a person to me.

He was an everyday guy. He talked about playing golf and how he had played with Groucho Marx. He really respected Groucho, who died shortly after the interview. He also talked about his love for beer. He said something that really bothered him was that there were too many people that didn't get the fact that 'Alice' was a character on stage. I was just getting that as he spoke.

He told us that one time while in the middle of a show this two hundred fifty pound madman jumped on stage to kick Alice's ass because the guy's girlfriend liked him. All the young girls loved Alice then. He had a girl's name but was nobody's sissy. He said he grabbed him by the shirt collar and the crotch of his jeans, picked him up over his head and threw him off the stage. Alice said "At the time I only weighed about a hundred twenty five pounds, don't get me wrong" he said "I'm not bad...but Alice is!" He also said that he could do almost anything on stage once the adrenalin started pumping.

In the spring of '75 everyone was talking about how Alice ripped a chicken apart on stage. So we had to ask him about that as well. "I'll tell you guys this, I'm a city boy from Detroit. Never went out into the country much so to me a chicken is a bird and birds fly. Someone put so to me a chicken is a bird and birds fly. Someone put the chicken on stage and I picked it up and threw it into the air. I thought it would fly to the back of the auditorium; it only made it to the fifth or sixth row and took a nose dive. The fans were trying to get a piece of it for a souvenir; THEY are the ones that tore the chicken to pieces!" That was cool hearing about it from Alice himself. He could only give us a few minutes because he was an hour ahead of us and had a show to get his head into.

Not long after the interview there was a story on the cover of Billboard Magazine with the headline "Alice Cooper Breaks Ribs On Stage During Concert." I saw it on Gary's desk. I asked if he had read the story, he said that he hadn't. "I guarantee you he finished the show before going to the hospital" I said with a smirk. I read the story and you know he did indeed finish that show. Not only did he finish the show, he did several encores.

To this day, that was one of my favorite interviews because he really opened up in it. He allowed our listeners to hear who he was and allowed them to get to know him a little bit.

I've had a long and somewhat successful career in radio. I've worked with a lot of talented and brilliant people in those years but of all of them Gary Guthrie's a stand out. Mainly because he wasn't just a great programmer on his way up, but because he believed in me and gave me the chance to do things and meet people

Chapter 15: All the Young Girls Love Alice

that I wouldn't have otherwise. We were what every Program Director and Music Director should be. We were a team, we were best friends and we thought alike. As Gary once said I was the perfect Pancho to his Cisco Kid. That's who we were like too, we were rebels, we bucked the system but in a charming and charismatic way. We took chances that other stations wouldn't have. We were creative, innovative and we made WRNO fun to listen to. That's the way radio should be.

Life was grand for me then. My career was going great and I was meeting and interviewing a lot of people I had admired for years. I had a great one bedroom apartment on the third floor of a complex in Metairie just outside of N'awlins and not far from the station. I built a hanging bookshelf that surrounded the living room. I had a 5 foot tall two by four post in each of the corners of the room and flat boards hanging from ropes. I used them to display over a thousand albums. The apartment was on the top floor. It had a forty-five degree ceiling with skylight widows just the right size and far enough apart for speakers. I put a chair on the kitchen table and put the speakers up in the windows. The sound was great and the look was even better. I had two or three bean bag chairs sitting around the living room with a couch and recliner so it was a serious listening room. I had some hellacious parties in that apartment.

I met a beautiful model named Kathy who lived in that complex. Her bathroom shared a wall with mine. I saw her all the time leaving for assignments and it seemed like she was always wearing a hat so I called her Kathy Tyler Moore. She was a health food nut and ate a lot to tofu which I called toyfud. I hated that stuff and she ate yogurt with no fruit, yuk. We worked out a code so when she came home with a date that she wanted to get rid of she would go to the bathroom and knock on the wall. Two knocks was I'm safely home and three knocks meant asshole in the apartment. If that happened I would go over and pound on her door yelling "Open this door, I know you have somebody in there." When she opened it I would walk in and head for her bedroom glaring at the guy with her. I'd tell her "I'll be in the bedroom. Get rid of him. We need to talk." Bar none they all offered to toss me out on my butt. She would just tell them that she could handle me. When they left we would laugh our ass off and drink a glass of wine.

I also hung out with one of the sales guys at the station, Dennis and his wife Beverly. He was kind of a nerd and she looked like Jennifer O'Neil. Why does that always happen? We would go out to dinner and movies; sometimes I took a date and sometimes just the three of us. Beverly and I teased Dennis as if there was something going on between us. It was all in good fun. I never thought much of it until one day when he came over as I was getting ready to go to the station. I was shaving or scraping my neck as I called it. I had the bathroom door open and Dennis was sitting on my bed. He started to bounce on the bed and said "Beverly and I are thinking about getting a new mattress, she like this one?" I lost it and he could see from my reaction there was really

Chapter 15: All the Young Girls Love Alice

nothing going on. Not only was she too good looking for him, she was also out of my league.

I decided to go home to Memphis for a vacation and gave Dennis a key to my apartment to keep an eye on it. When I returned as I was getting my key out of my pocket and walking toward the door I saw that it was already open and someone tore the hell out of it with what seemed to be a crow bar. I went running in hoping the albums were still there. They were of course all gone. The stereo was still there but the speakers were disconnected. It looked like they had been scared off.

I called the police and as they were doing the paperwork one of them asked me to step outside. I could hear him lock the deadbolt and then yelled "Ok, come on in." I couldn't get the door open. He opened it and said "Whoever did this had a key to your apartment and tried to make it look like a break in." I knew it had to be either maintenance or Dennis. I had an onyx pipe with a bowl that had a lion's head carved in it. When you took a hit the lion would glow red. It was gone with the albums as well as everything to put in the bowl, some Quaaludes and a few hits of window pain. I was pissed and yet hurt at the same time because I knew in my heart it was my friend Dennis that had ripped me off.

Dennis told me about a month later that he thought Beverly was going to leave him so he had a backup girlfriend. Beverly found out about the girlfriend and left him. That just proves what I've always said: whatever you think will happen, will. You make it happen as Dennis did by getting the backup girlfriend. Beverly told me she would have never left him if not for the girlfriend. She also said that it was indeed Dennis who had, as she put it, "Took your shit."

So you see, once again what goes around comes around. Dennis ripped me off. But I didn't have to do a thing about it. I Knew his karma was gonna get him. I lost a few albums but he lost the most precious thing in his life. The best thing about Dennis was Beverly.

Chapter Sixteen:
Memphis in the Meantime

It was 1976. Melissa Manchester had just released her third album, *Melissa*. I was familiar with her first two albums; *Home to Myself* and *Bright Eyes* from FM100 in Memphis and Radio Magazine. Although there were no hits from either of them there were a lot of good songs. She got a lot of airplay on album rock stations. She was compared to Joni Mitchell, Judy Collins and other female singer/song-writers of the day. At the time it was a well known fact that she sang back up for Bette Midler when Barry Manilow was Midler's Music Director.

I was doing 7-midnight and Gary asked me if I would like to interview Melissa. She was going to be in town to do a show that also included Boz Scaggs at The University of New Orleans. All the arrangements had been made to do the interview at Sea-Saint Recording Studio, owned by N'awlins music legend Allen Toussaint and his partner Marshall Seahorn. The session band at Sea-Saint was a group led by Art Neville (Aaron's brother) called the Meters. They opened for the Stones on their '75 tour and rumored to do the '76 tour as well (which they did). The Meters were also playing the show at UNO.

I got there early to meet Allen Toussaint at the studio and talked to him for quite a while about his career as singer, songwriter and producer before I went into the studio to interview Melissa. We talked about his recent success with Dr. John's "Right Place Wrong Time" and LaBelle's "Lady Marmalade." He had also played Key-

Radio Daze

boards and piano on Paul McCartney's *Venus and Mars* album which was re-corded at Sea-Saint.

When I walked into the studio to do the interview Melissa just took my breath away. She was so beautiful with long dark brown hair down on her shoulders and what a beautiful smile she had, warm and sincere. She was sitting at a white Baby Grand piano in a long black dress. As we talked she sang three songs including "Midnight Blue" as she accompanied herself on the piano. I had done other interviews with the artist playing the guitar, but never a piano. That was a first.

We talked about how she got her start much like Manilow, by writing jingles starting at the tender age of 15 or so. She talked a little bit about her family life and said her dad had been a musician at the Met. She told a story about how he was a tyrant when he drove and only knew two hand signals, one was c'mon around and the other meant, well basically I love you in its most primitive sense.

She also told me about this strange high school that she went to in New York. It was for students that wanted a career in the performing arts. A few years later it became clear to me that she had been talking about the High School of Performing Arts, the basis for the movie and TV series "Fame." She was real proud of the fact that she took a songwriting course at New York University taught by Paul Simon and then hit the club scene where she was discovered by Barry Manilow and Bette Midler.

Chapter 16: Memphis in the Meantime

In Manilow's "Could it be Magic" there's a line about Sweet Melissa... That was all pretty cool, we got along great and I really enjoyed talking to her. It was more of a conversation than an interview. I gave her a little background on the studio and the Meters. We cut up and laughed a whole lot during the interview. It was taped the day before the concert and played it back the next morning.

At the time her Label, Arista was new and in some markets (cities) including New Orleans, they didn't have a promotional staff. In those situations they would use the record distributor's promotional staff. In this case it was All-South Distributing. Their rep, Lenny Z was not a likeable guy. He had an inflated sense of self worth and was pretty much an ass in my opinion.

I ended up staying up all night editing the interview and getting it ready to air. I stopped off for some breakfast and headed out to the UNO campus to help get out the banners and other radio station paraphernalia. In addition to Melissa and the Meters, Boz Scaggs (who's 'Silk Degrees' album was a top seller), Mudcrutch, John Hammond and Heartwood were playing. It was going to be an all day event.

I was backstage talking to Melissa when Mudcrutch hit the stage. As we were talking she started looking around. She asked "Where's Lenny?" she explained he was her ride back to the hotel. Turns out ole Lenny had split and left her stranded on the football field at UNO.

Did I tell ya this guy was a class act? No phones, no cabstands and cell phones were well into the future. She was starting to stress a bit. It's not good to get stressed before you go out on stage. I told Melissa to relax, I would give her and Nancy (her manager) a ride back to the hotel. That seemed to relax her some.

As John Hammond was going on stage, I snuck away to burn one with some friends. I didn't know if Melissa would have wanted to go and I certainly wasn't going to say something stupid like "Do you get high?" If she didn't I was afraid she would feel unsafe riding back to the hotel with me. I felt I could drive safely even after smoking. She would still get there; it would just take a little longer. About half way through that set everything started to hit me. I had stayed up night, ate a big breakfast, a little work and a little smoke, I was ready to drop.

I found Melissa and told her I was going home, she looked at me and said "Oh you're leaving?" with a strange look on her face like I had just been caught cheating on her. I walked to my car, an orange VW Bug, and started to drive home. On the way home I was thinking about that strange look Melissa had given me. I thought back to the conversation we had earlier. We had been getting along so well at the interview. The day been going great, so what happened? Then it hit me. Holy Shit, I realized why she had that reaction. Her "ride" had dumped her twice that day. She couldn't ask someone for a ride to her hotel. I did a U-turn and headed back as fast

Chapter 16: Memphis in the Meantime

as that little bug would go.

I walked backstage just as Melissa was heading out to do her set. I apologized and told her I would be waiting when she came off stage. That didn't take very long at all because she only did two songs, the second being "Midnight Blue." She also asked that we not introduce her. She did want to check out the Meters set because of what I had told her the day before about opening for the Stones.

Boz Scaggs' Silk Degrees album featured one of Allen Toussaint's songs "What Do You Want the Girl to Do," along with hit singles "Lido Shuffle" and "Lowdown." I hated that I was going to miss his set.

Stoner's Limo Service

Melissa and Nancy were laughing hysterically all the way back about the VW "Limo" and stoned chauffeur. Don't cha just hate it when you think you are covering so well and you are really as transparent as a car salesman's sincerity? It was obvious. Anyway, I got them back safe and then I went home and slept until noon the next day.

The concert had been on Saturday. The next Monday as I was walking around the hotel lobby where I lived I

Radio Daze

saw Bob Robin, a friend who was an independent record promoter. He had an office in the building. He told me to be in his office at three o'clock that afternoon to receive a very important phone call. With him being a record promoter and me being the Music Director at the station the call could be from anybody. I tried to pry it out of him but he wouldn't say.

I was there a few minutes before three as requested. At three straight up the phone rang, he answered and said yes sir he's right here. As he handed me the phone I whispered "who is it?" He just gave me a motion to answer it. I said "Hello this is Mitch." On the other end of the phone came a somewhat gravelly voice that said "Hello Mitch, this is Clive Davis." "No seriously, who is this?" I asked. "This is Clive Davis. Melissa told me what you did after Lenny dropped the ball. She also told me you are from Memphis and we just happen to have an opening there. You showed me over the weekend you have what it takes to be a good promotion man. I have a round trip ticket to New York waiting for you at the New Orleans Airport. I want you to come and meet with my VP of Promotion, David Carrico, interested?"

Clive Davis is the Rock and Roll Hall of Famer, past President of Columbia Records who signed Paul Simon, Johnny Winter, Janis Joplin, Santana, Billy Joel, Aerosmith, Bruce Springsteen, Chicago, Blood, Sweat & Tears, and Pink Floyd. He was mentioned in Aerosmith's song from '79 "No Surprise," when Steven Tyler sings

Chapter 16: Memphis in the Meantime

"Old Clive Davis said he's surely gonna make you a star, just the way you are." He also took a little label called Bell Records and turned it into Arista and in the process made stars out of not only Melissa but Bette Midler and Barry Manilow as well.

Interested? You bet I am. I flew to New York City and met with Clive Davis and David Carrico. Now here's this little guy from Frayser High School sitting in a big Plush office in downtown New York City. I had lost the magazine but like the Jefferson's I was movin' on up. Hell, I impressed my own self. I got the job and went back to give notice at the station. I got all packed up and ready to move home and start my new job. I was returning to Memphis with my head held high.

A day or so before I was to leave, I got a call from David Carrico. He said the girl who had quit in Memphis to go to Warner Brothers Records had changed her mind and is staying with Arista. I have no job I thought. I had already quit at the radio station and now I have nowhere to go. I told David that I had already resigned at the radio station.

I started talking to radio stations in Memphis, New Orleans or anywhere else I could to try to find work. Within two days I got a call from LA. It was from the VP of Promotion of ABC Records. He told me that he had an opening in New Orleans. He also said that I had been "highly recommended." But he wouldn't say who it was that recommended me. I ended up going to work for

ABC who at the time had Joe Walsh, Steely Dan, Crosby & Nash, Rufus, The Four Tops, Jimmy Buffet, Jim Croce and a new artist that couldn't get arrested with a hit named Tom Petty. It was one of the greatest times of my life. I think it was Clive Davis who recommended me for that job. God bless him.

While I was with ABC Records I got to fly around the country and go to concerts to cater to our artist's every need. Luckily I catered to some really good people like Jimmy Buffett, Joe Walsh and Steely Dan. I had an expense account, an air travel card and talked to Program Directors and Music Directors all day long. I was living the life of Riley.

I got a new single in the mail one day and was ecstatic because I just knew all the top 40 stations would add it. It was by the two lead singers of a group that already had no less than twenty top 40 hits. As soon as I got it I headed over to WTIX, the #1 top 40 station in New Orleans. I just knew they would jump on it. They didn't. WTIX along with all the other stations said the duo were not a proven act without the rest of the group. "Are you kidding? They were the lead singers of the group. The group had hits because of them." I was determined to break the song, not because it was my job but because like Steely Dan's "Rikki Don't Lose That Number," I knew it was a hit.

I took my expense account dinner dollars to the secondary markets like Mobile and Little Rock. Those

Chapter 16: Memphis in the Meantime

guys never got treated to steak dinners just to listen to a song. Luckily I got it on at both KAAY in Little Rock and WABB in Mobile. They both reported their play lists to several of the trade magazines. I then headed back to New Orleans and went to several of the most popular Discos. I talked to the DJ's and gave them Steely Dan and Joe Walsh albums if they would just play the song in the club. I told them I would be checking to make sure they did.

That generated request at the stations and the secondary markets reporting got it into the trades. The New Orleans stations HAD to play it after that and once they did, it took off. It didn't stop until it reached the top of the charts. The song was "You Don't Have to Be a Star (To Be in My Show)" by Marilyn McCoo and Billy Davis of the Fifth Dimension. New Orleans was the first major market to add the song and I was proud that I had some small part of that record becoming a hit.

I gained a lot of respect when I was with ABC Records because I was so new to promotion and was the first to break a record that went on to become a major hit. Not long after that I flew to Dallas for a national promotion meeting. The subject of Joe Walsh came up. He wanted permission to record with the Eagles on Asylum Records and "The Shirts" didn't want to let him. His contract was coming up for renewal and my thought was if we didn't permit him to record with The Eagles he wouldn't continue to record his solo work with ABC. They didn't agree and when the contract was up he signed as a solo artist with Asylum and became the newest member of the Eagles. That was the first of many bad business moves by ABC executives.

I was flying from New Orleans to Little Rock a few weeks later. I went to the ticket counter and handed the agent my air travel card. He said "Well, uh...you're gonna need to pay cash for that ticket and we're gonna go ahead and keep this card" as he cut it in half with a pair of scissors. That was the beginning of the end for ABC Records. They were soon bought by MCA Records and most of the promotion staff was fired including me.

With no notice I needed to find some income and fast. I found a job spinning records in a disco in Fat City. That was twelve square blocks of nothing but clubs in Metairie just outside of N'awlins. I worked at a place called Fletcher's Nightery. I didn't like disco music but I needed the money.

To make the music more bearable I came up with a new drink. It was half Kahlua, half tequila and topped with 151 rum. You light the rum and shoot it down. Since you light it, I called the drink a Match McCrickin. After me of course, do one and disco didn't sound so bad. Do three and disco sounded damn good.

One night I was taking a break and went out back to smoke a joint with one of the bouncers. We were just about down to a roach. As we talked I was looking down the hill behind Fletcher's. The wind was blowing, it was a

Chapter 16: Memphis in the Meantime

beautiful night. There were a couple of clubs on the next street and their parking lot came up to the hill. The parking lot was maybe fifty yards away and packed full of cars.

I saw a couple of really attractive women dressed to the nines park their car and walk up to the door of one of the clubs. Just then a great big dude came stumbling out and put an arm around each of them. This guy looked huge, well over six feet tall and built like a linebacker. With a girl under each arm, they started walking back the girls car. I thought nothing of it, as I said there were blocks and blocks of clubs. Sometimes you would meet at a club and make the rounds. About halfway to their car the girls started screaming as he threw them down on the parking lot.

You never know what you will do at time like that. I always thought I was the kind of guy to look the other direction, to not get involved. I was wrong. After going through the trial with Pat I knew these girls would have scars that would never heal. No matter what he did to me, mine would. Besides there was a bouncer right there with me, he gets paid to beat people up. I just reached over and hit him on the arm with the back of my hand and said "Let's go." I started running down the hill shouting hey you Son-of-a-Bitch, that's my sister. I thought that would make it more personal. He looked up and saw us running at him and he already had two women to deal with so he bolted. I started laughing because no one had ever run from me before. I knew it was because I had the bouncer with me. As I laughed, I turned and looked back at him. He wasn't there. I was running at a mountain, calling him names with no backup. He was gone by the time I got to the girls. They were hysterical. He told them he was going to take them back to their car. He was going to put one in the front and the other in the back. Rape the one in the back and then trade places. If either one screamed, he would kill the other one. So they knew they couldn't let him get them to the car. They did the right thing. No one would have ever known had they not screamed.

I took them into Fletcher's and bought them drinks to calm them down. They drank them fast and said they just wanted to go home. They thanked me for my help and left.

Then, I went looking for Richard (or should I say Dick), the bouncer. "Where the hell did you go" I demanded. He said "I didn't want to lose my job for smoking behind the club." "Damn dude you can always get another job, a life? Not so much" I said in disgust. I never talked to him again, what a big wus.

I needed to find a real job and I needed to do it fast. I made a few phone calls. One was to my good friend Jerry Williams who always had his finger on the pulse of Memphis. If you wanted to know what was going on in the entertainment business Jerry was your go to man. He told me that Estelle Axton was looking for a national promotion man for her new label Fretone Records. She

Chapter 16: Memphis in the Meantime

was the "AX" of Stax, the label she co-owned with her brother Jim Stewart. With Jerry's recommendation, Mrs. Axton hired me. Little did I know that she was sitting on next year's People's Choice award winner. All I had to do is pick up the ball and run with it. "Long Distance information, give me Memphis, Tennessee"...I was on my way home and to a new gig.

I wasn't sure how long the job would last; they only had one record to work. I knew I wanted back on the air somewhere, but in the meantime I was headed to Memphis to do promotion for Mrs. Axton.

As I drove back to Memphis I turned on the radio and Buffalo Springfield's "On the Way Home" came on just as I was hitting the New Orleans city limits. The lyrics grabbed me "Now I won't be back till later on if I do come back at all ," My exact thoughts as I left Memphis with Rose.

I thought about how lucky I have been to have the career I have, to be able to meet so many people I have admired and listened to all my life. I also thought about how lucky I was to have loved the women in my life. How much I had gained from each of them being in my life. Well, except for Rose who seduced me, used me as her chauffeur to get to New Orleans and aborted my child. Not a big Rose fan.

I thought about Betsy and how much she believed in me in high school and how proud she would be of me now. I wondered if we would be married now if she had lived. I wanted to see Dad again, he wasn't getting any younger and I had wasted a few years not talking to him. I really didn't care that much about seeing Mother but I did want to see Bob, his family and my brother and sisters. I thought about how much I had learned from my childhood. That even though it was a hard life at home, it made me who I am and I'm pretty happy with the way things turned out.

I couldn't help but think of what I was leaving behind too, the friends I had made in New Orleans like Miranka, Aloma from Homa, Beverly and Gary Guthrie. All of them had become close friends. I had learned through my travels in radio to look ahead, not back. Looking at what you are leaving is always sad but looking forward to where you're going is exciting.

To be honest, most of what I thought about was Pat. I still loved her and that would never change. There would be other loves in my life but going through her addiction and rape with her created a bond for me that would never be equaled. I wanted so bad to see her but she was doing great now both personally and professionally. I was torn as to what to do. Should I try to see her or just let it go?

The first thing I wanted to do when I got home was to get a cheeseburger from Huey's where Pat and I used to go. It was right around the corner from our old apartment. I'm a hopeless romantic so I thought even if I don't

Chapter 16: Memphis in the Meantime

go see Pat I can at least visit with her memory in our old neighborhood and eat at "our place." It had been a while since I had a Huey's cheeseburger. Even now when I do, I still think about Pat and the good times we had on South Rembert. Yeah, there were some bad times too but the good thing about loving someone is that you always seem to remember the good in them. To me, Huey's will always be our place.

To be continued...more stories about radio, records, the joy of fatherhood and the agony of divorce.

Mitch McCracken writes articles on Memphis Entertainment and Classic Rock for the *Examiner*. He also writes freelance for the Memphis Daily News. Mr. McCracken has also published stories on the missing Ampex 361 Recorder from Sun Studios, and several on legendary West Memphis, AR radio station KWEM. In September of 2011 he signed with MVP3 Entertainment to produce a movie based on Radio Daze.